MW01254742

Barefoot Theology

For Bonnie with much love & gratitude!

Barefoot Theology

A Dictionary for Pilgrims, Priests, and Poets

RACHAEL A. KEEFE

Rachael A. Keefe

WIPF & STOCK · Eugene, Oregon

BAREFOOT THEOLOGY
A Dictionary for Pilgrims, Priests, and Poets

Wipf & Stock
An Imprint of Wipf and Stock Publishers
199 W. 8th Ave., Suite 3
Eugene, OR 97401

www.wipfandstock.com

ISBN 13: 978-1-62564-075-8

Manufactured in the U.S.A.

Dedicated to four incredible people without whom this book might not have been writeable.

Alice Owen Williams (1931–2013) was an English teacher extraordinaire who told me to keep writing, especially poetry, and then offered her friendship and encouragement for decades.

Linnea Johnson (1946–2013) was my poetry professor and friend who revealed to me the complexities of writing poetry and the freedom that comes from self-acceptance.

John H. Williams (1937–2011) was a remarkable pastor whose strength of conviction and unwavering support have shaped my own way of being in the world more than he ever knew.

James E. Loder (1931–2001) was an extraordinary professor who gave me the language of faith and embodied the astonishing joy of life in the Spirit.

Contents

Acknowledgments

Countless people deserve thanks for their role in the writing of this book, but I will try to be as specific as I can. Thank you to Erika Sanborne for the idea and for your numerous comments, edits, and suggestions along the way. Thank you, also, Tim Thomas for your willingness to read anything I sent your way and for offering your own special brand of enthusiastic encouragement. Elaine Thomas, thanks for your advice on musical metaphors even though I didn't include them since my musical abilities are extremely limited. Thank you, Merle Jordan, for your early readings and continued support. I am also grateful to Bonnie Haase for her careful reading and suggestions for revisions. I also owe a special thanks to my Facebook friends who responded to informal surveys and helped determine the content of this book.

Author's Note

I chose *Barefoot Theology* for the title of this book for a couple of reasons. One is that I have an image in my head of Moses removing his sandals so he can get a little closer to God. If being barefoot is what it takes to walk on holy ground, then I'm in. I prefer to be barefoot whenever possible and even sometimes when it is not practical. The feel of a beach's sun-warmed sand under my feet on an early spring day or chilly fall day restores my soul like nothing else. I also think that the shoes-off, relaxed approach is really the best one for this book.

While the idea of a non-dictionary, theological dictionary is inspired by the works of Frederick Buechner, the poetic slant is uniquely mine. Poetry paints images or twists something familiar into an unexpected shape. Theology is quite similar, really. Studying theology can completely change one's perspective and alter one's life. Using poetry to define theological words presented some challenges. Of course, none of these poems are truly definitions and not all of the words would be considered theological, but they all have something to say. Some may evoke emotions while others provoke them. This is the beauty of both poetry and theology.

You may notice some classic forms of poetry and some more contemporary ones, though I hope that what you most notice is the thought or the image captured in the words. You will also hear hints of the theologians who have most influenced my thinking—Martin Luther, Paul Tillich, Jurgen Moltmann, Frederick Buechner, James Loder, and Kenda Dean among others. I am grateful to them for their work and words that have challenged and shaped my own.

Now take your shoes off, wiggle your toes in some warm beach sand, and enjoy *Barefoot Theology*.

Prologue

When the Lord saw that he had turned aside to see, God called to
him out of the bush, "Moses, Moses!" And he said, "Here I am."
Then he said, "Come no closer! Remove the sandals from your
feet, for the place on which you are standing is holy ground."
Exodus 3:4–5

THEOLOGY

I often dream of walking
across a desert of dry sand
intending to reach an ocean
of such a brilliant blue
that I can almost taste its
coolness on my dry tongue

When I look down at the grains of sand
they are not miniscule stones
they are words
thousands upon thousands of words
just for me to know and use
without limit

Prologue

If I pick them up they disappear
yet when I take off my shoes
the desert loses its heat
and the words call my name
reminding me not to hurry
the journey is more sacred
than the waiting waters

I suddenly feel the weight of all I carry
my arms are full of books I've read
or want to read
while on my back are the worries
of others piled up like so many prayers
I've never let go

I set down the books
watching as they grow deep roots
and sprout into a tree of knowledge
with fruits of science, math, ecology,
medicine, economics, poetry,
and every other topic known and studied

At the very top is a glowing fruit
of theology filling me with longing
I forget about the startling blue ocean
waiting for me across the desert of words
in my efforts to reach the wonder of theology

The tree is not climbable
branches move out of my reach
until I give up in exhaustion
then a few fruits fall into my lap
allowing me to hear the words
of the sand calling my name

I'm halfway across the sand
when I notice the fruits from the book tree
have made a necklace of shining
beautiful segments to hang around
my neck without weight
calling attention to the burden
I still carry

Those worries for others
piled on my back nearly bending in half
I stand up and they slide off
snapping together like Legos
creating a bridge to the azure waters
from right under my feet

Those waters wash right over me
the pieces of the necklace I wear
snap together on their own
to become the dazzling brightness
of theology I had so wanted

Suddenly I am back on my feet
surrounded by a garden that grows
people as well as flowers
no one is allowed to wear shoes
because all ground is holy
and we must be able to hear
the words that come to us

When I wake up the pieces of this dream
fade into my day but I know for sure
that God is best approached from
many directions with bare feet
exposed to the Word that
comes to us

A

For God so loved the world that he gave his only Son, so that everyone who believes in him may not perish but may have eternal life.
John 3:16

AGAPE

God loves without condition
remaining steadfast when people choose
anything and everything else to worship
God waits for each one of us
without ever giving up

Jesus walked this world and spoke of peace
reaching out to the unreachable
healing the untouchable
opening the eyes of those blind
to holy ways

When the world could tolerate
this Love Incarnate no longer
the man was crucified
so that we might live more fully
knowing God's unconditional love for us
revealing the Christ in humanity

making us all equal when seen
through Sacred eyes

To speak words of love is not enough
our call is to live in the Word of Love
recognize the value bestowed on us
by the One whose breath we breathe
in whose likeness we are made

Let us set aside all our conditions,
rules, and regulations
we think keep us safe
yet only mask our fears and hide us
from ourselves and our neighbors
let us step into the arms patiently
waiting for us
arms wide enough
to embrace the world

God thinks you and I are worthy
of Jesus' life, death, and resurrection

May this truth startle us into living
Love without conditions
well beyond our usual limits

As for you, the anointing that you received from him abides
in you, and so you do not need anyone to teach you. But as his
anointing teaches you about all things, and is true and is not a lie,
and just as it has taught you, abide in him.
1 John 2:27

ANOINTING

Hands
press my head
barely touching
unbearably heavy
light enough to blind
reveals everything

Sight
restored to closed eyes
memory tickled
familiar scent
ancient knowing
casts out

Demons
Mary had seven
a nameless man had legion
I am somewhere in the middle
until the oil
the body broken

Communion
imperative then
almost impossible
I am split open
to the core
asunder no more

Barefoot Theology

                              Healing
                     silence burst into being
                    chaos ordered
              suddenly I am
          exhausted
     clinging to shadows

    Wholeness
          fractured still
               almost within reach
                    in my self
                         free from demons
                         I am

                         Life
                    begun again
               the first time
          vulnerable to touch
     strong enough
to bear freedom

There will be signs in the sun, the moon, and the stars, and on the earth distress among nations confused by the roaring of the sea and the waves. People will faint from fear and foreboding of what is coming upon the world, for the powers of the heavens will be shaken. Then they will see "the Son of Man coming in a cloud" with power and great glory. Now when these things begin to take place, stand up and raise your heads, because your redemption is drawing near.
Luke 25:28

APOCALYPSE

polar ice caps melting slowly
ocean waters eating our shores
seasons blending into each other
storms increasing in voracity
foreboding fills those who pay attention

war consumes lives faster than we notice
violence grabs young lives daily
prisoners push the limits of confinement
homeless people grow in numbers everywhere
despair exhausts those who work for change

these could surely be signs of the end
though I'm not looking for the Son of Man
because these things are not the work of God
global warming, war, poverty are all
works of human hands

destroying ourselves and our world may appear
to match the description of Armageddon
but if we obliterate ourselves
will our redemption still draw near?
perhaps it is better to change our ways
than to bring about an apocalypse
not yet meant to be

But now, apart from law, the righteousness of God has been disclosed, and is attested by the law and the prophets, the righteousness of God through faith in Jesus Christ for all who believe. For there is no distinction, since all have sinned and fall short of the glory of God; they are now justified by his grace as a gift, through the redemption that is in Christ Jesus, whom God put forward as a sacrifice of atonement by his blood, effective through faith.
Romans 3:21–25

ATONEMENT

Whether you side with Irenaeus or
Augustine, Ablelard or Calvin, Grotius
or Aulen, don't mistake their thoughts for
infallible Truth. Facts can be fictitious
when based on a mystery so profound
as to fuel debates for two thousand
years. To contemplate Christ is to confound
the human mind trying to understand
why our God would care enough to become
the Incarnate One—living and dying
and rising again—so none would succumb
to sin and death (through lack of choice). Defying
laws and history, reason and tradition,
Jesus improves the human condition.

Augustine, Anselm, Luther and Wesley
highlighted satisfaction in their schemes,
while whom, exactly, Jesus redeems
defines the atonement philosophy
of Calvin, Barth, and Edwards. I will not
be so bold as to say they are all wrong,
though, perhaps, a new question should be sought.
Maybe, just maybe, running headlong
from Original Sin to Crucifixion
missed the very real possibility

of God's seeing the world differently.
What if sin wasn't God's motivation?
What if it's deep love for humanity?

When it comes right down to it, I am not
very interested in anyone's atonement theories.
Now do not let this thought get you distraught.
You don't need to change. I raise my queries
simply to point in another direction.
Scripture tells us that God so loved the world . . .
amazing love offering salvation
to all who believe—new life unfurled
in a single act, overwhelming sin
and death. How do we yet focus on who
is saved rather than the Gate that lets us in?
Forgiveness and Love, Hope and Grace, are true.
Jesus' love is meant to free us from ourselves
not trap us on theologians' bookshelves.

B

There is one body and one Spirit, just as you were called to the one hope of your calling, one Lord, one faith, one baptism, one God and Father of all, who is above all and through all and in all. Ephesians 4:4–6

BAPTISM

font
    pool
        lake
            river
                immersion or aspersion

                infant
            child
        teen
    adult
parental proxy or public proclamation
makes no difference

God knows you
loves you
claims you as beloved
before you know yourself

we need this sacrament of water and spirit
to remind us of our holiness

water from the Jordan River or straight from the tap
    poured from a shell or sprinkled with a rose
        or completely submerged
            does not impact the promise

                your conversion or your parent's desire
            brings you to the same place
        of water and word
      of forgiveness and grace
    of welcome into
the body of Christ

Barefoot Theology

You shall not make wrongful use of the name of the Lord your God, for the Lord will not acquit anyone who misuses his name.
Exodus 20:7

BLASPHEMY

why do we forget what we believe in intense moments
words are not meaningless even when uttered in
pain or anger, fear or exasperation
how common it is to use God's name in vain
without thought, purpose, or consideration
of any line we might have crossed
and what could be waiting on the other side
there is a reason Jesus became the Incarnate Word
maybe we ought to try and live more respectfully

The Lord bless you and keep you; the Lord make his face to shine upon you, and be gracious to you; the Lord lift up his countenance upon you, and give you peace.
Numbers 6:24–26

BLESSING

open hands
healing broken spirits
building hope after destruction
Love

Blessing

new promise
encouraging change
trust growing in place of fear
Hope

Blessing

holy gift
unbinding human hearts
unexpected joy enhancing life
Grace

C

In the beginning was the Word, and the Word was with God, and
the Word was God. He was in the beginning with God. All things
came into being through him, and without him not one thing
came into being. What has come into being in him was life, and
the life was the light of all people. The light shines in the darkness,
and the darkness did not overcome it.
John 1:1–5

CHRISTOLOGY

Jesus is God
    fully human
    fully divine

    beyond our understanding
        well within holy capacity
        to out-reach human comfort

        the extent to which we focus on this mystery
            determines the place of Christ within our theology
            higher or lower probably doesn't matter all that much

            we could argue endless hours over the importance
                of this doctrine or that when determining just
                who Jesus is, was, and will be

Although, for me, it comes down to
the leap that faith requires
the jump into joyful unknowing

> Pilate spoke to them again, "Then what do you wish me to do with the man you call the King of the Jews?" They shouted back, "Crucify him!" Pilate asked them, "Why, what evil has he done?" But they shouted all the more, "Crucify him!" So Pilate, wishing to satisfy the crowd, released Barabbas for them; and after flogging Jesus, he handed him over to be crucified.
> Mark 15:12–15

CRUCIFIXION

Did Jesus have to die?
The question is so common
that novelists and Hollywood
have attempted alternative answers
and explanations to alleviate
the discomfort.

The high priests involved that day
would agree that Jesus needed to go
and Pilate wanted to be done with
his work for the day and did not care
what happened to Jesus so long as
the disgruntled crowd dispersed
and he could get home to supper.

Who was responsible?
The Pharisees and Sadducees who were
threatened by Jesus and his teachings?
The Roman officials who had the power
to set Jesus free in spite of the charges?
The crowd that had gathered with high
hopes for an entertaining afternoon?
The deplorable state of humanity

and its sinful separation from God?
The God who became Incarnate
just to die for the sake of the world?

Some of all these things and more
beyond my understanding.
Mostly, I want to say it was politics.
Jesus created a problem with his
words and deeds upsetting the status quo
to the point of threatening those in powerful
positions who would rather remain unshaken.

Yet, of course, Jesus's death was more
because God took charge and turned
what should have been the end of a charismatic
movement for change into the very change
itself echoing down through centuries
with the promise of freedom and grace,
hope and life, for those who choose
to follow the way of One who gave his
life for the sake of the world.

Nothing ended on the cross that day
unless we let ourselves get caught up
in maintaining the status quo
without ever thinking about what
the One who hung on a cross
really meant for us who would
take up his name.

Barefoot Theology

> Meanwhile the church throughout Judea, Galilee, and Samaria
> had peace and was built up. Living in the fear of the Lord and in
> the comfort of the Holy Spirit, it increased in numbers.
> Acts 9:31

CHURCH

A building that reaches back in time
Pulling forth nostalgia and yearning
For a time when pews were full
Paint wasn't peeling
the pipes didn't clang
and people made worship a priority

Traditions built on events half remembered
Become sacred acts unchanged
And unchangeable no matter
Who walks in or out

A people who call on Christ
In all things with some reluctance
to embrace freedom and forgiveness
and follow where the Holy One leads

Not a building
Or Traditions
Or a stubborn people

Church is a vision of holiness
not made by human hands
Where two or more are gathered
In prayer
In praise
In spirit

In truth
Welcoming all
In or out of favor
Where whose we are matters
Far more than who we are
and love speaks louder than
we have never done it that way before

> Therefore confess your sins to one another, and pray for one
> another, so that you may be healed. The prayer of the righteous is
> powerful and effective.
> James 5:16

CONFESSION

Holding onto to sin smothers the human spirit
like cancer in a smoker's lung
Denial
Depression
Despair
add more weight
as days pile up

Speaking the truth lets in airy light
and possibilities take shape

God will hear you if you whisper in the darkest night
yet you may not hear the word of forgiveness
alone with yourself

Find another who knows the Word
who can bear your shame
and speak aloud the absolution
you desperately need

Our God does not need our words of pain or shame
to give us the forgiveness Christ already gives
we need to name our demons
out loud or they will grow wild in our denial

Then we are free to breathe deeply of grace proclaimed
set down our cancerous burdens
and be healed

You did not choose me but I chose you. And I appointed you to go
and bear fruit, fruit that will last, so that the Father will give you
whatever you ask him in my name.
John 15:16

CONVERSION

Once I wrote to You as a child, frightened and alone.
I claimed not to know the "ways of the world."
Since then, I have learned . . .
Only too well.
I have seen anger and destruction,
Felt the horror of emptiness.
The traps I fell into were set in my innocence
And sprung in my resentment.

I am an adult now.
No longer can I claim naïveté.
Nor can I say that I do not know You.
You have come into my life,
Saved it, actually.
I tried to throw it away,
You gave it back with gentle force.

Yet still, I question.
So much sadness, so much hatred.
For a while I was a part of it—
Of refusal and denial.
As I said, I am no longer a child
And You give me life.

The questions I raise are not of disbelief,
More a of desire to understand.
Why do so many question Your power

Barefoot Theology

And Your love?
You gave your life . . .
What more do they need?
These things tug and pull me from within.

The sadness and anger I once held for myself
Have become larger, less selfish.
I long to heal the world's wounds.
I have been a victim of its pain and suffering.
Now I am being healed by Your presence.
I feel Your call;
You draw me closer,
You ask me to serve.

I am no magician.
I cannot change my humanness.
Doubts and fears keep me from wholeness
Yet, You call me.
My life is ensnared in worldly nets;
You offer freedom and direction.
Sometimes I am haunted by the child I once was
And You tell my heart to quiet.

Why?
After the violence I have seen
And the pain I have both inflicted and acquired,
Why do You love me and want me?
I have laughed away Your gifts,
Lied and denied until I almost lost it all.
You forgive me—then, now, and always.
There are so many more worthy,
And You choose me.

My guilt is great,
My burdens heavy,

You offer Your assistance.
The world sinks into its own,
You raise me up.
I was once imprisoned
And You drew me out
To show me life.

I see now and am thankful.
My reluctance is not for lack of knowledge.
I am afraid.
I've been caught before,
Denied You many times;
I don't want it to happen again.
This is where I fail You:
Doubt, anger, and want keep me fragmented.

These things I say and do,
What are they to You?
You must be hurt
When I repeat my wrongs again and again,
Your love surrounds me.
Keep me with you always;
Prevent me from losing my way.
Let me choose You with trust and assurance
As You have chosen me with love.

For now we see in a mirror, dimly, but then we will see face to face. Now I know only in part; then I will know fully, even as I have been fully known. And now faith, hope, and love abide, these three; and the greatest of these is love.

1 Corinthians 13:12–13

COVENANT

dripping, crackling melting snow
fills January thawing sounds
breaking the silence of deep winter
a few days of promise
lighting dark days
bringing hope make me think

of other oaths made after other storms
Noah's gift was wrapped in a multi-colored bow
and assured to last generation to generation
the earth will not flood again
unless we do it ourselves

Abraham and Hagar strangely
imparted with the same direction
to look to the stars
after pain beyond measure
they would have progeny
who would twist love into hatred as the years add up

Moses, Aaron, and Miriam danced
across desert sands with a People in tow
desperate to reach the Promised Land
which remains not quite attained

many, many others followed in these footsteps
until they culminated in fulfillment
between an upper room, a cross, and an empty tomb
a sacred covenant excluding no one
even those who turn away

warm days in January, a temporary warmth
still spring always follows winter
the sunrise happens with startling regularity
as covenant goes beyond promise
larger than the particularity of you or me

an invitation to dance
extending beyond the joy of communion
through the pain of sin and sorrow
in spite of what we do
to the planet, each other, or ourselves

Love never ends.

D

Do not fear, for I am with you; I will bring your offspring from
the east, and from the west I will gather you; I will say to the
north, "Give them up," and to the south, "Do not withhold; bring
my sons from far away and my daughters from the end of the
earth— everyone who is called by my name, whom I created for
my glory, whom I formed and made."
Isaiah 43:5–7

DIASPORA

My garden grows a little wild
with weeds and violets taking over
the golden marigolds bloom
next to white the impatiens
with pink lilies behind them
and hosta greens to the side
behind the little fence
exactly where I planted them

A careful observer will see
a spot of pale pink hiding
in the cluster of hosta leaves
last year's petunia planted itself

in a new spot without asking permission
blooming happily out of place

A closer look at my lawn
reveals remnants of gardens past
with smiling pansies growing
here and there well beyond the boundaries
adding color to the grass
when I wait too long to mow

Out past the backyard fence
a strange mix flourishes in unplanned
clusters of bright tiger lilies, white violets,
Queen Ann's lace, and other flowers
I never planted creating
their own garden with abandon

Funny these flowers that grow
where they choose with blatant
disregard for fences, plans, and designs
the clover and grass don't seem to mind
pansies and petunias taking root here and there
nor do the marigolds object when the wild
violets crawl up close
and the azalea bush is content to shelter
the mint from hungry slithering things
You can take this as a reflection of my poor
gardening skills or you can ponder the life
of plants and flowers who defy rules and
expectations without a thought
of judgment or condemnation

We would do well to listen to the flowers
grow where we are planted
not fearing to grow where we land
reveal the beauty we were given

Barefoot Theology

to enhance that of our neighbors
and stop worrying so much
some of us grow better outside garden fences

Do not be conformed to this world, but be transformed by the
renewing of your minds, so that you may discern what is the will
of God—what is good and acceptable and perfect.
Romans 12:2

DISCERNMENT

Clouds
nearly black
cloak the sun
they rush from horizon
to shore across a churning
sea bringing defiant winds painful hail
excessive lightning streaming rain mind-numbing thunder
I created this storm that rages
through my life watched it
gather strength knowing it
would hurt me
I changed
nothing
ignored intuition
stubbornly focused on
my having my own way
until the first startling thunder shocked
me into stillness recognizing my reckless needless
flight into chaos God would have
me do otherwise if
I'd just be
still and
know

Go therefore and make disciples of all nations, baptizing them in the name of the Father and of the Son and of the Holy Spirit, and teaching them to obey everything that I have commanded you. And remember, I am with you always, to the end of the age.
Matthew 28:19–20

DISCIPLE

called
by One
who loves all
no conditions
yet those who respond
live the challenge to love
and serve neighbors and strangers
bearing wisdom, grace, love, justice,
and hope into an unhappy world
to follow Jesus truly assures change

The Lord upholds all who are falling, and raises up all who are
bowed down.
Psalm 145:14

DIVORCE

I stand in between
neither where I have been
nor where I will be
just where I am

Between
    youth and age
    doubt and faith
    movement and stillness
    pain and hope
    married and unmarried

Between the mirror and the reflection
    I see
        an undiscovered life
        a reluctant intake of breath
        a change in direction yet to be taken
        the sharp edges of broken dreams
        the ambiguity of separation

I wait in the gloaming
    while the long drought of summer
        gives way to the threat of autumn frost
            and the promise of winter storms
                spring remains unconceived

Barefoot Theology

Trees stand
    and leaves fall
        out of sync with seasons past
            while I wait for grace to fall like autumn rain
                to wash my sins away into the cold,
                    dormant darkness of winter
                        to be reborn in the warmth of the sun

E

He is not here; for he has been raised, as he said.
Matthew 28:6

EASTER

He is not here. He's risen, as he said.
Such simple words of truth and mystery,
of promise fulfilled—One no longer dead.

An empty tomb marked, unexpectedly,
the beginning of a new way of being.
Such simple words of truth and mystery

can lead us to a new way of seeing—
ourselves and our neighbors equally loved.
The beginning of a new way of being

ripples through centuries, naming beloved
all who seek to worship and live in truth,
ourselves and our neighbors equally loved.

Easter is not the foolishness of youth.
It's evidence of God's amazing grace.
All who seek to worship and live in truth—

may we see the risen Christ in each face.
"He is not here. He's risen, as he said."
It's evidence of God's amazing grace,
of promise fulfilled—One no longer dead.

Therefore I endure everything for the sake of the elect, so that they may also obtain the salvation that is in Christ Jesus, with eternal glory. The saying is sure: If we have died with him, we will also live with him; if we endure, we will also reign with him; if we deny him, he will also deny us; if we are faithless, he remains faithful—for he cannot deny himself.
2 Timothy 5:10–13

ELECT

All Christians who live
in faith, serving God
in word and in deed.
They persevere when
others lose hope.

The certainty
of God's steadfast
love sustains them.
There's no limit

in numbers.
Only God
knows who's saved.

Could be
every

One . . .

You must understand this, that in the last days distressing times will come. For people will be lovers of themselves, lovers of money, boasters, arrogant, abusive, disobedient to their parents, ungrateful, unholy, inhuman, implacable, slanderers, profligates, brutes, haters of good, treacherous, reckless, swollen with conceit, lovers of pleasure rather than lovers of God, holding to the outward form of godliness but denying its power. Avoid them! 2 Timothy 3:1–5

ESCHATOLOGY

no
one
knows the
hour or day
when Christ will return
why study Last Days when present
days are challenging enough for most folks to live through
humanity can't seem to live without violence and war, poverty
and hunger, distance from
our Creator seems a natural drive even when
we want otherwise still we are
given grace how
soon will the
wisdom
come
near

While they were eating, Jesus took a loaf of bread, and after blessing it he broke it, gave it to the disciples, and said, "Take, eat; this is my body." Then he took a cup, and after giving thanks he gave it to them, saying, "Drink from it, all of you; for this is my blood of the covenant, which is poured out for many for the forgiveness of sins." Matthew 26:26–28

EUCHARIST

sacramental gratitude
ritual remembrance
inviting grace

an old ski cabin full of retreating adolescents
a weekend of fellowship and sleep deprivation
closing worship on couches around a coffee table

Cool-Aid and Goldfish crackers out of place
the coffee mug and pitcher went round the room
each poured out red juice while naming a blessing

until the last when the cup overflowed
Unexpected elements but the words were spoken
Jesus met us in that space of serious searching

transforming left-over snacks into a sacred meal
a familiar ritual into a sacred experience
awkward teen-agers into disciples

Consubstantiation
Transubstantiation
Spiritual Presence
Meal of Remembrance

Barefoot Theology

Mostly it's a mystery

Just bring yourself to the table
participate in the promise
taste and see . . .

And Jesus came and said to them, "All authority in heaven and on earth has been given to me. Go therefore and make disciples of all nations, baptizing them in the name of the Father and of the Son and of the Holy Spirit, and teaching them to obey everything that I have commanded you. And remember, I am with you always, to the end of the age."
Matthew 28:18–20

EVANGELISM

When Mary agreed to Gabriel's proposal
      she brought Jesus into the world
      making her story his story

When we take our own place in this narrative
we are to do the same—
      bring Christ into the world
      make our lives a testimony
      to God's presence here and now

Making disciples is not the goal
but the outcome of Christian living

Our words alone cannot fully reveal the Word
      our lives speak more loudly
      than any preaching ever will

The psalmist's wisdom still holds true—
      if the words of our mouths
      and the meditations of our hearts
      along with the works of our hands
      are acceptable in the sight of Lord
then making disciples will be no problem

Proselytizing might add to our numbers
though full pews mean nothing
       if we do not embody a contagious witness
       igniting desire in others to be baptized
       and take their place in the on-going Story

F

Jesus said to him, "If you are able!—All things can be done for the one who believes." Immediately the father of the child cried out, "I believe; help my unbelief!"
Mark 9:23–24

FAITH

Questions.
Always more questions
seldom more answers—
 When children are murdered
 or war rages for decades
 or super storms destroy without warning
 or cancer claims another life
 or bullied children kill themselves
 or too many people ask
Why does God let this happen?

It's hard to believe in an
omniscient, omnipotent, omnipresent,
all-things-are-possible kind of God who loves
yet human beings mess with creation
and blame the Giver for the Gift
when it is misused and overlooked.

Barefoot Theology

Quantity is not relevant—
   remember the mustard seed
      and the mountains in need of moving
         or the woman who touched a garment
         drawing on power she expected
           or the leper cleansed
           and returned to give glory
              or the blind man whose eyes
              opened on an impossible world

              Quality might also be irrelevant
              given the doubts that shape our beliefs
              it's about choosing the impossible odds
              that God still loves the world
              including the stubborn, fragile, willful
              creatures who bear the divine image
              more than they know or understand

In the face of tragedy or sickness or pain
we demand to know what this God of ours
has done and why so much is left undone
we should take a breath, deep and full,
remind ourselves that God has done great things
You and I are created and shaped by grace,
given the breath of holiness
and loved beyond measure
not to sit back in doubt, blame, or shame
to do nothing more than weep or complain

In a moment of clear honesty
we can see the steadfast love of God
present in all of creation
even where human hands cover it over

Doubts can lead us to questions
and pain can lead to anger
before an answer comes
when we want to know why
the world is such a mess and
what God has done about it,
look in the mirror
the answers will greet you there

It is impossible now to hold silence
Lord, I believe; help my unbelief.

> Then God said, "Let us make humankind in our image, according to our likeness; and let them have dominion over the fish of the sea, and over the birds of the air, and over the cattle, and over all the wild animals of the earth, and over every creeping thing that creeps upon the earth." So God created humankind in his image, in the image of God he created them; male and female he created them.
> Genesis 1:26–27

FEMINIST

Born of woman—first daughter then mother
yet neither is she. No one to teach
her how to live, to breathe, to be her sex.
Woman, no doubt, beautiful in body—
mother of all—life given in birth;
nothing remaining for her daughter.

Not a thing remains for her daughter—
no hope, no love—nothing from her mother
and none from her mother before. Birth
after birth and no woman to teach
her the sweet secrets of her body
or the power dormant in her sex.

The power dormant in her sex
was lost in time unseen by a daughter
born of a woman with a shapeless body,
concealed in the dark cloak of mother.
She is alone. Nothing to give or teach—
no way to live unless through birth.

No way to live unless through the birth
of another, a child of her sex,
a girl-child to learn and grow and teach

her how to be a woman—daughter
first then growing into mother,
removing the cloak from her body.

She will remove the cloak from her body
and claim all life denied at her birth,
breaking the silence between mother
and child, releasing the female sex.
The ancient tree will bind this daughter
no more. She will learn and grow and teach

her child to learn and grow and teach
the others the beauty of the body.
The first woman will live in this daughter
and come alive again with every birth
to follow. No more cloak to cover her sex,
her power, her life, her love, her mother.

Woman now teacher—able to give birth,
uncover her body and free her sex,
love her daughter and embrace her mother.

Come to me, all you that are weary and are carrying heavy burdens, and I will give you rest. Take my yoke upon you, and learn
from me; for I am gentle and humble in heart, and you will find
rest for your souls. For my yoke is easy, and my burden is light.
Matthew 11:28–30

FORGIVENESS

never a question
of earning or of
deserving more a
basic need to let
go of pain, anger
and resentment to
find a new freedom to love and be loved, to know joy
and grace and the abundant life that opens up when a
hand is no longer a fist and the spirit relaxes enough to
embrace new possibilities but unless you are God there
is no question of forgetting just of letting go, moving on,
reconciling when possible sometimes it's a daily activity
directed at others
or ourselves as we
try to accept and
live what Christ
poured out for us
that doesn't change
when we forget to
ask for the gift that
takes the shape of
the One who gives it
and makes us yearn
to go and do the same

For God's foolishness is wiser than human wisdom, and God's weakness is stronger than human strength.
1 Corinthians 1:25

FOOLISHNESS

short, fragile pickets
around the volleyball court
sturdy stockade at the harbor's edge
solid, low wooden walls
      to mark the beach club's beginning and end
      rickety, already tilting rows running to the ocean
      to keep the private
      beach touch-free until spring

fog and night combine to swallow the red sun
the moon rises with a star
a crisp crescent—laughing in the sky
I am tempted to knock down the fences—
run wildly, trampling them
who would think to put fences in the sand?

G

But now thus says the Lord, he who created you, O Jacob, he who formed you, O Israel: Do not fear, for I have redeemed you; I have called you by name, you are mine.
Isaiah 43:1

GOEL

One
who stands
fearlessly
in the face of pain
bearing witness to suffering
never letting go until all are redeemed, gathered in,
reclaimed, renamed, reborn to abundant life in a beloved
community where
none are forgotten, unwanted, unclean, or unseen
as all join together to face
injustice, making
the weak strong
bringing
hope

How beautiful upon the mountains are the feet of the messenger
who announces peace, who brings good news, who announces
salvation, who says to Zion, "Your God reigns."
Isaiah 52:7

GOSPEL

centuries have passed since Jesus' feet were on any mountain
yet he gave new meaning to "good news"
embodied salvation
could not have said more clearly to God's people,
"Your God reigns"
a couple millennia of years have squashed
the life out of those beautiful feet

the only feet remaining to climb mountains to bring good news
are yours and mine, and my feet are pretty ugly
yet when they stand on ground made holy
by the message they carry
they are transformed with the rest of me
it's time to climb mountains of ambivalence and apathy
and proclaim the love of Christ for all the world
without qualification or apology

salvation
forgiveness
grace

can make all feet beautiful while breathing new life
into the ancient message

our God reigns

this is the Good News
thanks be to God

Barefoot Theology

The law indeed was given through Moses; grace and truth came through Jesus Christ.
John 1:17

GRACE

pain slowly easing
    after a burden born too
long—forgiveness owned

    possibility
        unfolding, transforming old
    selves into new life

        fragile fluttering
            of hope's first rising after
        long, dormant darkness

            the ripple of love's
                unmistakable touch now
            changing perspective

                releasing shame and guilt
                    after long captivity
                to breathe deeply of life

Rejoice always, pray without ceasing, give thanks in all circumstances; for this is the will of God in Christ Jesus for you.
1 Thessalonians 5:16–18

GRATITUDE

Without a doubt we are called to give thanks to the Lord
    often this praise does not flow readily from our lips

Except maybe in the obvious moments
    Like
        Sarah
        Hannah
        Elizabeth
            after the birth of a son in years beyond the possibility

        A woman bent over
        Mary of Magdala
            A man possessed by Legion
                after Jesus cast out the evil spirits—
                one, seven, or many

    Job
    Jonah
    Paul
        from a life restored, the belly of a whale,
        with opened eyes

    Moses
    Miram
    David
        after deliverance from the enemies' hands

Barefoot Theology

A Samaritan woman at a well
A nameless woman who anointed Jesus
A Son of Timaeus
    after living water, oil and tears, mercy received

In the moments after new life,
salvation, healing, forgiveness, mercy—
    any unexpected encounter with grace—
spontaneous emissions of thanksgiving
might tumble from our mouths
    now think of those ten lepers Jesus sent on their way to healing
    only one of them returned to offer thanks
    the other nine just went on their way

It is one thing to give thanks after the storms have passed
    and the rainbow hangs in the cloudless skies
It's quite another to sing in the midst of the earthquake, the winds,
or the fire
    to pay attention at all times to what is good
    to notice the ordinary things
    to know that we are blessed even in chaos
    to take time to find that still, small voice
    to know that God is here and now
        calling your name,
        offering abundant life
        waiting

Who does not want impossible blessings
    freedom from personal demons
        an end to suffering
            release from oppressive hands
                transformation and healing?

        It's too easy to walk away
        like those nine and never look back

Truth be told, I want to be the leper who returns, always
moreover

I want to dance the way David danced
uninhibited, free
rejoicing in the Lord

Such joy and thanksgiving
would make all the difference

H

Then I saw a new heaven and a new earth; for the first heaven and the first earth had passed away, and the sea was no more. And I saw the holy city, the new Jerusalem, coming down out of heaven from God, prepared as a bride adorned for her husband. And I heard a loud voice from the throne saying, "See, the home of God is among mortals. He will dwell with them; they will be his peoples, and God himself will be with them; he will wipe every tear from their eyes. Death will be no more; mourning and crying and pain will be no more, for the first things have passed away." Revelation 21:1–4

HEAVEN

In memory of Eleanor Morgan (1917–2010)

hours from death
already less alive
yearning for release
from what had become
constant pain in a body
well used and worn out
she was ready to go
home to a Lord she
had known her whole life

"Tell me about heaven,"
she said in a whispery voice,
eyes closed, ready to see
whatever I described
taken aback with this innocent
request, I took a breath
wiped a tear and started
with what I knew

>You will be free from pain
>and be able to walk again,
>run and play tennis with
>your beloved

>It'll be beautiful there
>like a warm beach with fresh
>ocean breezes or a meadow
>with singing birds

>And you'll be able to eat again
>whatever you like
>chocolate, pizza, and ice cream

"Tell me more," she said with longing.

>You'll be with God
>and filled with peace
>far beyond the love
>you've known here

When I looked up from my prayerful state,
she had drifted into sleep with a smile on her face

I don't know what she thought as I reached
for words to describe what I hoped would ease
her last hours

Barefoot Theology

What comes after this life is a mystery
with a few glimpses and promises
offered in scripture
Yet, I spoke truth when I painted Gram
a picture of freedom and happiness
she so deserves after a lifetime of love
and service in Christ's name

Her last words were "Thank you"
whispered shortly before she died
I'd like to think they were the first words
she heard when she met
her God face to face

And this is the judgment, that the light has come into the world, and people loved darkness rather than light because their deeds were evil.
John 3:19

HELL

dedicated to all people who suffer with unrelenting mental illness

I have stood at the gates of hell
listening to the tormented souls
plagued by visions of demons,
death, and destruction.
These poor souls will be saved
from eternal damnation
because they suffer in this life
with illness beyond the reach
of modern medicine.

I've also heard the confessions
of those who are tortured by
shameful memories of pain
inflicted on them by others
who take delight in destroying
innocent young lives with evil deeds.
Heaven will open wide one day
to receive these who were blinded
to the Light before they knew
where to look.

As for those who steal hope
and life with their actions,
I'd like to think that they
will know an eternity's
worth of suffering being

cast away from a God who is love.
Though I wonder if, they, too,
would receive forgiveness
if they repented of their evil ways.
I wouldn't grant it, but God is more
gracious and understanding than
I can ever hope to be.

When it comes right down to it,
hell exists where God does not.
Many of us think we have been there
because in excruciating pain
God seemed to be missing.
Maybe this is just a glimpse
of what it would be like to live
in the total absence of love,
an absolute darkness where
no Light ever shines.

Even now, with all the suffering
and pain I witness, I cannot
imagine such a place.
I pray that no one ever does . . .

But where shall wisdom be found? And where is the place of
understanding?
Job 28:12

HERMENEUTIC

if new knowledge is really what you seek
your chances of success are not so bleak
      know from whence you look
      no gobbledygook
this propaedeutic rhyme lets wisdom speak

Barefoot Theology

> Create in me a clean heart, O God, and put a new and right spirit within me. Do not cast me away from your presence, and do not take your holy spirit from me. Restore to me the joy of your salvation, and sustain in me a willing spirit.
> Psalm 51:10–12

HOLY SPIRIT

The very breath of God
blowing where she wills
advocating for justice
descending like a dove
bringing peace

The fire of faith
kindling flames of passion
igniting innovation
burning away fear
transforming lives

Another aspect of God
who touches our lives
often without our knowing
until we look back
and see the change in direction

May the God of hope fill you with all joy and peace in believing,
so that you may abound in hope by the power of the Holy Spirit.
Romans 15:13

HOPE

Remembering Sandy Hook—December 14, 2012

I watch the sun rise on cold ocean shore.
Brilliant scarlet streaks across the horizon
as if light has been cut away from darkness.

Waves, winds, and the cries of gulls
break the turbulent silence of my thoughts.
Restless and grieving, sleepless and yearning,
I wait for a new day.

I cannot make sense of the senseless—
war, violence and gunshots echoing endlessly.
Innocents slaughtered. Politicians ranting.
People divided. This is not good enough,
not nearly good enough.

Into the wind I scream the names of God I know
Jesus! Allah! Adoni! Vishna! and a thousand more . . .
Can You not hear? Do You not know? Do something!

As I stand breathless in anger,
the sun bursts out of the red-tinted night
lighting an unexpected moment of stillness.

Waves, wind, and gulls whisper words I know—
Peace! Salam! Shalom! Shanti! and thousands more.

Barefoot Theology

In the light of morning I know the truth—
My hands, my heart, my life are needed
to bring Sacred Love into a shattered world.

After a night of wrestling,
       I go limping into the day
              with hope reborn.

He has told you, O mortal, what is good; and what does the Lord require of you but to do justice, and to love kindness, and to walk humbly with your God? Micah 6:8

HUMILITY

breathing deeply
calming fear
quieting the voice that says, "don't"
moving your feet
to walk with a neighbor
or a stranger
who shouldn't carry burdens alone
not for any reason
other than you can make a quiet difference
without needing recognition

one display of kindness
a single act of justice
changes you as much
as the recipient

breathe more deeply
give thanks
you are an agent of grace
walking with Christ

I

Certain elders of Israel came to me and sat down before me.
And the word of the Lord came to me: Mortal, these men have
taken their idols into their hearts, and placed their iniquity as a
stumbling-block before them; shall I let myself be consulted by
them? Therefore speak to them, and say to them, Thus says the
Lord God: Any of those of the house of Israel who take their idols
into their hearts and place their iniquity as a stumbling-block
before them, and yet come to the prophet—I the Lord will answer
those who come with the multitude of their idols, in order that I
may take hold of the hearts of the house of Israel, all of whom are
estranged from me through their idols.
Ezekiel 14:1–5

IDOLATRY

we are much too practical these days to bow down
before statues but the idols of our hearts lead
into darkness before we know what's happened or
recognize what we've set up on a pedestal
our lives become consumed by the gods within us
until we look around and see that we have gained
nothing that matters and lost all that had meaning

food drugs tattoos anger alcohol prestige loss
medication sex work money prejudices
weight memories piercings regrets appearance fear
hatred greed gambling power love self-absorption
gluttony bullying ignorance rejection
intolerance self-hatred vanity desire
pain popularity adrenaline and more

when we find ourselves worshiping at such flimsy
altars with gods far too small to respond to our
deepest yearnings forgiveness is just a small step
toward a God who invites us to come bearing all
our idols and iniquity even if they
are more than a multitude when we turn to God
estrangement ends with God grabbing hold of our hearts

> So God created humankind in his image, in the image of God he
> created them; male and female he created them.
> Genesis 1:27

IMAGO DEI

On midsummer's eve, when the world is wrapped in magic,
all the children of the earth gather in the dreaming place.
Mysteries call louder on this night than on all other nights.
Whispers carried on ocean and mountain breezes lead
children to gather in the dreaming place.

They laugh and dance and splash in the magic surrounding them.
The moon rises higher, children quiet in the whispering winds
and ask the questions of their hearts.

One small girl stands and says,
My daddy doesn't look like my mommy and
I don't look like either of them.
So who does God look like?

The answers are quick and from all around.
Some of us together.
    All of us.
        None of us because maybe there is no God.

        Silence.

The winds themselves laugh and dance wildly though the gathering.
Then they speak with the voice of One.
    You ask what the Holy One looks like?
        Do you not know?
            All of you bear my likeness.

Children wait, breath held, still.

I am the first light of morning;
I washed some of you in its soft fairness.
I am the pureness of deep night;
I wrapped some of you in this sacred darkness.
I am the fire of the setting sun;
some of you have this burning in your hair.
I am the richness of the soil—
red, brown, yellow, and black—
as are many of you.
I am the depth of the ocean;
some of you wear these greens,
blues, and grays in your eyes.
I am the warmth of the summer sun
found in all your smiles and laughter.
I am the stillness of winter snow
resting within each of you.

What does the Holy One look like?
I am all the colors of the earth.
I am the softness of early spring
      and the wildness of thunder.
My reflection is in the ocean
      and in your eyes.
I am the first light of day
      and the last dark of night.
I am the power of the wind
      and the gentleness of misty rain.

Look for me in yourselves,
      each other,
            and in all creation.
      Do not miss the holy in the setting sun,
            the purple twilight,
                  the darkest night,
                        or the brightest noonday.

Barefoot Theology

Wherever you are, I am.
I am in your laughter and your tears.
I am in waking and dreaming.
If you want to know what the Holy One looks like,
you will see me wherever you turn.

The winds quiet and the skies grow lighter.
The little girl laughs
as the winds play through her hair.

The children drift away from the dreaming place.
Each takes a little of the magic of midsummer
and wakes bathed in the first light of day.

J

Rejoice with those who rejoice, weep with those who weep. Live in harmony with one another; do not be haughty, but associate with the lowly; do not claim to be wiser than you are. Do not repay anyone evil for evil, but take thought for what is noble in the sight of all. If it is possible, so far as it depends on you, live peaceably with all.
Romans 12:15–18

JUSTICE

A Chinese friend frequently hears "Go back where you came from!"
She is hurt more than she lets on but pretends to be numb.
How can hatred be based only on what we see?
Lord, have mercy.

An African neighbor has hateful words sprayed on his house
just because he wants to live in peace with his spouse.
When ugliness and fear step in where grace ought to be,
Christ, have mercy.

Young ones kill themselves when the bullies go unchecked
because no one can see the life that hateful words have wrecked.

How can we not learn this lesson when it's shown so painfully?
Lord, have mercy.

Homeless women, men, and children hide in the shadows
we walk in a hurry—compassion is something fear overshadows.
For all the times we cannot tolerate, "This could be me,"
Christ, have mercy.

Muslims are suspect even when they are life-long citizens
of a country founded on religious freedom and welcome of aliens.
Is it impossible for us to accept someone who worships differently?
Lord, have mercy.

Black men and women crowd our jails with frustrated rage
as our laws uphold racism and so few recognize this outrage,
while others spew such hatred and violence freely and publicly.
Christ, have mercy.

Women are paid less and targeted more for perceived weakness
and, for some, abuse is still inflicted when there is a lack of meekness.
Why are laws so slow in changing what should not be?
Lord, have mercy.

The elderly are victimized by scammers who readily take what is
    not theirs
and it's a shame when this happens with no one around who cares
enough to help and protect ones so vulnerable who deserve safety.
Christ, have mercy.

Gay men are beaten on the streets of cities known for their
    acceptance—
headlines and news stories report witnesses and their helpless
    tolerance.
For all the moments of learned helplessness and studious apathy,
Lord, have mercy.

Bigger walls and more border protections to keep illegals out
when all they want is a chance at a better life and, without a doubt,
they would find it here if there were such a thing as legal hospitality.
Christ, have mercy.

Surely the day is coming when fear, violence, hatred, and greed
will cease and loving kindness is the response to all human need.
Are we not called by God to rejoice and live peaceably?
Lord, let us be your mercy.

> You did not choose me but I chose you. And I appointed you to go
> and bear fruit, fruit that will last, so that the Father will give you
> whatever you ask him in my name.
> John 15:16

JUSTIFICATION

When the sun brightens an azure sky
and the earth bursts into bloom
I have no trouble believing
      my life is sacred
      your life is sacred
      all life is scared
I am sinless in the eyes of my God
      a gift freely given
      from a hill called Calvary
      a tomb long empty
Mine for the receiving at birth
      or baptism
      or confirmation
      or conversion
      or those moments when my heart
            quietly echoes the ancient centurion
            "Lord, I believe; help my unbelief."

Yet, when the sun is lost in cinereal skies
and the earth reveals harsh edges
belief comes hard
      Who am I to be gifted with such grace?
      Why would God so honor the ambivalence of humanity?
      What in this broken, desperate world is worthy of Christ?
            Those who claim his name most loudly
            throw hatred and judgment at innocent
            victims who have done no more than suggest

a different way of living
or being
or praising
or loving
and the question becomes a plea
Help our unbelief!

Mostly though I walk under cloud-scattered skies
where light and shadow dance together
faithfully displaying forgiveness and need
knowing all are equally gifted with possibility
offered long ago because the entire world
is so loved
into abundant life
a gift not to be received lightly
one to be honored in the process of becoming
the whole person reflected in the eyes of our God

K

Many Samaritans from that city believed in him because of the woman's testimony, "He told me everything I have ever done." So when the Samaritans came to him, they asked him to stay with them; and he stayed there two days. And many more believed because of his word. They said to the woman, "It is no longer because of what you said that we believe, for we have heard for ourselves, and we know that this is truly the Savior of the world." John 4:39–42

KERYGMA

No one really thinks of her as a preacher
since her identity as a sinner
is much more interesting
and captivating
five husbands and one more
leave her alone at a well in the middle of the day
while everyone else is hiding from the desert sun
she comes to draw water
when she won't touch another

She didn't count on Jesus being there
to offer her a drink that would make her
way more than a nobody to be avoided
rather a somebody with passion and power
to be heard in spite of her lowly status
as a woman living in sin

Jesus filled her with living water
and she poured it out
all over everyone she met
and they believed because of her Word
a village worth of folks came to Jesus
because this outcast woman had something to say

The words she used don't much matter
because she was filled with a greater Word
that could not be ignored
imagine that passion
conviction
conversion

No less than Peter or Paul
Silas or Stephen or Timothy
she spoke truth drawn
from a bottomless well
which transformed her
and all those who heard her story

When's the last time a preacher's
words had that kind of power
to change lives in that very moment?
Why do we settle for less
than what those Samaritans heard
that sent them running to see for themselves?
Where is the Living Water
that strengthened that nameless woman

when the words pour forth from our pulpits
and wash away so little?

If we really want that early church preaching
then maybe we should get ourselves to the well
with all the sinners who thirst for Living Water
and aren't afraid to drink in the presence
of the Word who comes to us
in the fullness of grace and truth
until our testimony pours out
new life
abundantly

For now we see in a mirror, dimly, but then we will see face to
face. Now I know only in part; then I will know fully, even as I
have been fully known.
1 Corinthians 13:12

KNOWLEDGE

Clouds balanced perfectly over a rising sun
creating a brilliant display of light and color
unseen before or since

Waves washing gently over a rocky beach just
after the storm has quietly moved out to sea
while pink twilight slips in

Bright green leaves tipped, here and there, in autumn color
while summer plays on and few notice the changes
pointing to cooler nights

Sudden laughter surprising the grief stricken heart
sooner than anticipated, bringing healing,
welcomed with gratitude

Good news coming shortly after horror, calming
fears, giving new perspective to the hardened soul
making joy possible

Breathing in silent stillness as thick fog blankets
the night, temporarily halting all movement,
rejoicing in peace

Seeing violence, injustice, evil, oppression
all around without giving up all hope and faith
while bearing witness

Choosing to find evidence of the Creator
in creation, to seek Christ in humanity,
to shine with holy light

L

How long, O Lord? Will you forget me forever? How long will you
hide your face from me? How long must I bear pain in my soul,
and have sorrow in my heart all day long?
Psalm 13:1–2a

LAMENTATIONS

A biblical book about the fall of Jerusalem
poetically rendered to remind the faithful
how keenly sorrow and grief can touch a people

Beyond the book, though, it is good to cry out
to God when nothing can break through the pain
of loss or shame or guilt or heartbreak

Tears shed honestly pleading with God to hear
the need of those bowed down with suffering
and beg for circumstances to change
can bring clarity, relief, and the possibility
of recognizing that God has not abandoned anyone

The most common laments contain some version
of "Why me?" or "How long?" these questions

seldom receive an answer any different from
the response given to Job

Fortunately, God attends to the cries of those
who suffer, forsaking no one

The Christ who shared the fullness of human life
and uttered his own laments will enter into ours
until we quiet ourselves enough to hear
that still, small voice whispering a new song

In the beginning was the Word, and the Word was with God, and the Word was God. He was in the beginning with God. All things came into being through him, and without him not one thing came into being. What has come into being in him was life, and the life was the light of all people. The light shines in the darkness, and the darkness did not overcome it.
John 1:1–5

LOGOS

the hush of the world newly blanketed with early winter snow
whispers of rain falling on fresh spring leaves
echoes running through summer heat
the crackle of autumn's first frost

the voice compelling the artist to paint
not stopping until the canvas reveals truth
a sculptor's vision of what lies hidden
needing to be freed piece by piece

a prayer unmistakably answered
the call that can only be responded to
with a life of service
like the prophets of old who could only say,
"Here I am; send me."

at the core of these moments is the Word
become flesh who lived among us
and lives still embodying Wisdom
speaking to us in the silence
transforming us in moments of stillness

sometimes hard to hear through
the clutter of words

Barefoot Theology

we use so casually
the Word of God speaks
if we dare to listen

Pray then in this way: Our Father in heaven, hallowed be your name. Your kingdom come. Your will be done, on earth as it is in heaven. Give us this day our daily bread. And forgive us our debts, as we also have forgiven our debtors. And do not bring us to the time of trial, but rescue us from the evil one. For if you forgive others their trespasses, your heavenly Father will also forgive you; but if you do not forgive others, neither will your Father forgive your trespasses.

Matthew 6:9–15

THE LORD'S PRAYER

a model of prayer meant to be a guide
has become the mark of Christians everywhere
      across denomination, sect, and culture
      these words are part of worship—
         public and private

we may be bold to say them
especially when we aren't listening
we are asking for more than we know

fortunately for us
God pays more attention
and has yet to answer this prayer in full
      the Kingdom has not yet arrived on earth
      when we encounter trial and evil
      we are not left alone
      nor are we held to the measure of forgiveness
      we are forgiven even when we hold grudges

maybe we should be more mindful
of the lesson Jesus intended
      to offer a prayer that honors God
      and asks honestly for what is needed

Barefoot Theology

      recognizing our limitations
      knowing God has none

then we should pray with intention
to the One who hears our prayers
and answers them

M

My beloved speaks and says to me: "Arise, my love, my fair one, and come away; for now the winter is past, the rain is over and gone. The flowers appear on the earth; the time of singing has come, and the voice of the turtledove is heard in our land. The fig tree puts forth its figs, and the vines are in blossom; they give forth fragrance. Arise, my love, my fair one, and come away."
Song of Solomon 2:10–13

MARRIAGE

we held hands, my beloved and I
made promises to care for one another
to share laughter and tears
forgiveness and grace
strengths and weaknesses
to bring all of ourselves to this
sacred moment
standing before friends and family
asking God to bless and bind our relationship
then we stepped into our wedded life

Barefoot Theology

we hold hands now, my beloved and I
whispering, "Come away with me"
in moments of quiet celebration
offering comfort in grief
encouragement when hope slides away
never forgetting the blessing we received
the day God joined us together
for a lifetime of never letting go

one day the beauty of spring
will be a shadowy memory
after adventures through seasons
stormy and gentle
all with my beloved saying,
"Arise my love, my fair one,
come away with me"
always hand and hand
blessed with Grace

Go and learn what this means, "I desire mercy, not sacrifice." For I have come to call not the righteous but sinners.
Matthew 9:13

MERCY

Assist those in need
Bind up the wounded
Care for the widow and orphan
Defend the defenseless
Encourage the hopeless
Free the captives
Give strength to the weary
Harbor the refugee
Inform the ignorant
Join the activists for justice
Kindle hope in the lost
Lift up the down trodden
Move those who are stuck
Nurture the weak and lonely
Open the eyes of the blind
Provide food for the hungry
Question the powerful
Resist apathy and ambivalence
Shelter the homeless
Treat all with kindness
Uphold justice for the oppressed
Victimize no one
Work for peace in the world
eXalt in the joys of another
Yearn for righteousness
Zealously live in compassion

"This is my commandment, that you love one another as I have loved you."
John 15:12

MINISTRY

The Way of Jesus may not always be
as smooth as the road to Emmaus
    when hearts and eyes open wide
sometimes the path is lost in wilderness wandering
with hungry, thirsty people
    until the direction becomes clear again
I choose to follow because I do not go alone
    a great crowd of witnesses lend me
    courage, wisdom, and strength

    Like Moses I may stammer out refusal
    while taking off my shoes
        to stand on the sacred ground of leading God's people
        even when fear and confusion prevails
        until water flows from rock and bread falls from heaven
        and the Promise Land is in view

    Like Miriam I will sing out loud
    and dance as though no one sees
        when the People of God celebrate life, rejoicing
        in abundance, recounting blessings previously unnoticed
        gratitude fills us all with the need to praise God
        for the transformation in us and around us

    Like Abraham I will sacrifice almost anything
    if God has need of it
        even when I am impatient and think I know a quicker way
        I trust that God will forgive my foolishness

and the stars will continue to shine
until the People of God are more numerous

Like Sarah I will laugh when God
makes the impossible possible
 and let my doubts be reshaped by grace
 a reminder that no one is empty when God is present
 rivers flow in dry lands, the barren give birth,
 and even those who sit in total darkness
 will see a great light

Like Mary of Magdala I bear witness to the healing,
to the empty tomb
 to the Christ who knows my name
 and the number of hairs on my head
 no one is insignificant, no life too small, no life forgotten
 by the one who bids us all to follow

Like the Samaritan woman I will stand
boldly in the noontime sun,
 drinking living water from a well with no end
 offering a drink to all who thirst for more than what is
 when religion is not spiritual enough

Like Peter I will be impulsive and impetuous,
wanting to be the best
 while stumbling over my humanity
 when I forget Christ's divinity
 needing to be saved from drowning
 in the limits of my being
 proclaiming Jesus all the while wanting everyone to know
 Christ's great love for the world even when I forget

Like so many others whose names I do not know
 who lived faith fully enough to keep faith alive for me

and you who want to follow even now when the Way
is simple in a world full of complications

I am making this journey through valleys
and across mountain tops
welcoming any who wish to travel in the company of sinners,
tax collectors, outcasts, and saints
who know the need for repentance,
forgiveness, grace, and healing
at the hands of the One who bids us follow

Let us walk together on holy ground

Then the eyes of the blind shall be opened, and the ears of the deaf
unstopped; then the lame shall leap like a deer, and the tongue
of the speechless sing for joy. For waters shall break forth in the
wilderness, and streams in the desert; the burning sand shall
become a pool, and the thirsty ground springs of water; the haunt
of jackals shall become a swamp, the grass shall become reeds and
rushes. A highway shall be there, and it shall be called the Holy
Way; the unclean shall not travel on it, but it shall be for God's
people; no traveler, not even fools, shall go astray.
Isaiah 35:5–8

MIRACLE

I lived in a painful place
between an ending and a beginning
uncertainty disturbed my sleep
most mornings would find me at the beach
before the sun even thought of rising
I'd sit on the damp sand
huddled around my coffee mug
waiting to see if the sun would rise
and bring light to my personal darkness

    one morning I looked up through my
    self-absorbed tears to see a spot of color
    a brilliant red streak spreading across the horizon
    reaching north to south and widening to touch
    the morning stars still dimly shining
    this crimson line pulled the sun up
    out of the black ocean waters
    and lit the night on fire

Barefoot Theology

exploding colors across my vision
orange, yellow, red beyond description
surrounded the sun as it transformed
darkness into light

> when I looked away
> I began to see
> life all around me
> greeting the day with enthusiasm
> seagulls grabbing crabs
> pipers running through tidal pools
> other sojourners seeking the quiet
> beauty of ocean's dawn

> > I felt it then
> > the quiet assurance
> > of God's loving presence in the midst of my pain
> > opening my eyes to the wonders always
> > present even when I cannot see

> > > this morning revelation may not
> > > rival biblical healings or
> > > water into wine
> > > though for me it was transformation
> > > water flowing through the desert of my life
> > > my sight restored as hope filled me
> > > the temporary paralysis of pain lifted

the sun rises everyday
tides flow high and low
the world around us teams with life
to notice and give thanks
might just be the
Holy Way

N

One of the scribes came near and heard them disputing with one another, and seeing that he answered them well, he asked him, "Which commandment is the first of all?" Jesus answered, "The first is, 'Hear, O Israel: the Lord our God, the Lord is one; you shall love the Lord your God with all your heart, and with all your soul, and with all your mind, and with all your strength.' The second is this, 'You shall love your neighbor as yourself.' There is no other commandment greater than these."
Mark 12:28–31

NEIGHBOR

Arbitrary hatred and fear
hardens hearts and ruins lives
while we sit safely in our pews
surrounded by plaques and stained glass
reminding us of where we have been
which might be where we are
with our locked doors and ancient hymns
believing we welcome all into our fellowship.

Barefoot Theology

The reality of who we are tells another story.

Sanctuaries were meant to provide asylum, refuge, safety
for anyone who came knocking and seeking
asking for safe haven amidst the tribulation
surrounding the body of Christ out in the world.

When's the last time our pews held more than the usual
cluster of congregants come to worship and sing praises
to a God who calls us beyond boundaries and borders?

Homeless, runaway, mentally ill, refugee, elderly
Muslim, Jew, Hindu, Wiccan, Buddhist,
African, Asian, Russian, Afghani, Indian, Arab,
gay, lesbian, bisexual, transgender, queer
victim, veteran, hungry, evicted, convict, enslaved,
black, white, red, yellow, brown
lonely, lost, hopeless, desperate, helpless, confused,
divorced, addict, disabled, grieving,
guilt-ridden, ashamed, suicidal, or
any other kind of human being that stirs
discomfort when they come too close
and want to sit in our pews and share in our fellowship
even if they call God
by another name and want only sanctuary for a little while
it remains us and them.

One Lord. One faith. One Baptism. One table. One loaf.
All may come and eat
and be satisfied.

Someday, maybe . . .

Jesus told a story about a man beaten and left for dead
even by the religious sorts who walked right by
the unexpected, supposed enemy showed mercy
two thousand years ago and we forget
the call to show mercy
more often than we remember.

The question of "who is my neighbor?"
has been asked and answered.

Blessed are the merciful
for they shall receive mercy.

Barefoot Theology

> So I say to you, Ask, and it will be given you; search, and you will
> find; knock, and the door will be opened for you.
> Luke 11:9

NEED

Lord of Travelers and Pilgrims,
You have called me to a new path.
I ask your guidance.
This move is like no other;
I'm going home
and I'm bringing myself.

    God of Grace and Light,
    shine on all that I am
    and all that I am not.
    Let your wisdom fill me as
    I choose
    what I leave and what I bring.

        Holy One,
        May Courage be the first thing I pack
        so I leave no room for Fear.
        Next, let me choose Acceptance to
        fill the corners where Bitterness tends to hide.
        I want Beauty to come with me;
        I no longer need Hatred for myself.
        Layer Healing through all I pack
        to remind me that I do not need Helplessness.
        Love, of course, will fit nicely into all
        the places Anger used to fill.

Creator God,
May your hand be especially in these next—
Trust doesn't fit so easily; but I must
make room by leaving out Isolation.
Intuition needs lots of room,
so Denial stays behind.
I need also make room for Sexuality;
it fits better than Shame.
Let me put Balance
in Chaos' place.
May I also pack enough Wholeness to live fully
and leave Pain which binds me to death.
And, finally, there is Freedom. I have enough room
for this now that I don't need Victim-space.

You are the Lord of Life—
Even as I pack these things,
I hold them out to you.
Shape them into the woman
You have created me to be.

Lord of today,
    This is a move made in Hope,
    toward a future filled with Light.
    I am moving—though slowly, sometimes.
    The journey is hard even at its beginning.
    Be with me as I walk away from here
    that I may find you there—
    as I come home to my self, Your Self.

O

Then Jesus said, "Father, forgive them; for they do not know what they are doing."
Luke 23:34

ORIGINAL SIN

We're always looking for a culprit
someone to blame for poor choices
mistakes made on impulse
or under control of emotions
beyond our grasping
need for expression or relief

Whatever it is, we are at a loss
to explain what drives us to deceit
destruction or despair

Was it Adam, Eve or the serpent
who brought sin into the world?
Surely it was not me or you or
anyone we know who has made
spectacularly bad choices

causing pain all around
breaking relationships
and destroying hope

It's not exactly original to point a finger
in another's direction to avoid
responsibility, consequences for actions
we wish we'd not taken

If we are made in the image of God
then the capacity to choose good or ill
is part of the divine stamp we bear
so what does it matter whose fault it is?

In Christ we are made whole
awash with forgiveness, grace, and love
even before baptismal waters remind us
whose we are

Maybe it's time do something original
and acknowledge our culpability for
those things we do that we ought not
and those we do not do that we ought
and live in the grace we proclaim
expecting others to do the same

Perhaps then we will be more willing to love
our neighbors and ourselves
believing, living, and breathing
Christ's love for us.
Our sins are forgiven.
May we all go and sin no more.

> O Lord, who may abide in your tent? Who may dwell on your holy
> hill? Those who walk blamelessly, and do what is right, and speak
> the truth from their heart . . .
> Psalm 15:1–2

ORTHOPRAXY

a schizophrenic man once asked
if I would bless his shampoo and conditioner
so that the evil spirits in the water
could not take his brain away
he had not showered in weeks

no class covered this question
my denominational affiliation
doesn't support blessing any thing
reserving this for living creatures,
preferably human ones

this tormented man who asked
in earnest desperation
and more faith than I had witnessed
for quite a while
surely his need was stronger
more important than words on a page
or classroom teachings

I asked if he would use his products
if I blessed them so the demons
couldn't touch him and he
agreed wholeheartedly to shower
as soon as he returned home

in the chapel with those bottles on the altar
a man filled with delight by my side
I felt silly as I asked God to bless
shampoo and conditioner for that gentleman's use
until such peace as I have seldom seen
quieted the man as he asked me to bless him, too

with anointing oil still on my hands
in an empty chapel on a blustery fall afternoon
I knew for sure just who had been blessed that day
what a gift to give and receive—
do what is right
before we know it
all shall be well

P

And may the Lord make you increase and abound in love for one
another and for all, just as we abound in love for you. And may he
so strengthen your hearts in holiness that you may be blameless
before our God and Father at the coming of our Lord Jesus with
all his saints.
1 Thessalonians 3:12–13

PAROUSIA

She cried silent tears while I sat with her
several minutes passing before she spoke,
"Jesus is going to come back and
my heart is broken, not holy."
Not understanding her despair, I waited.
"I am not holy enough to please him."

Had her pain not been so clearly real,
I might have been tempted to laugh.
Instead, I moved next to her,
took her hand in mine,
and prayed:

Lord Jesus, thank you for this day,
this time to begin again
and learn from one another.
Heal our brokenness—
in our bodies,
in our hearts,
in our minds,
in our spirits.
Let us live more holy lives
so when you come again
you will be pleased to call us
your children.
Amen.

The young woman, wiped her tears
and turned to me with a smile.
"Thank you! I don't know when Jesus
is coming, but he is! And now I think
I will be ready and so will you."
She stood up to go.
Before leaving she turned and faced me
to say, "I'm bi-polar but not crazy.
Jesus is coming someday. And he loves you
just like he loves me. Don't forget."

No, I don't think I will.
No one should, really.
Perhaps if we all lived lives more holy,
believing in Christ's promised return,
we'd find ourselves with less brokenness
in our bodies,
our hearts,
our minds,
our spirits.

Come, Lord Jesus, come.

Jesus said to him, "No one who puts a hand to the plow and looks back is fit for the kingdom of God."
Luke 9:62

PASSION

leaves dancing in the wind
waves dashing to the shore
inviting you to do the same

a moment of conviction
setting a soul a-fire
    tossing
        turning
            yearning

            unsettling enough
                to stand up
                sit in
                shout out
                protest with silence

                lay down life
                for those who suffer
                    in hands who know better

           take it up again
              to bear witness
              shine in darkness
            speaking truth
against power corrupted

when the purpose is
    justice
    freedom
    grace
    love

for neighbor or stranger
    who has no voice
      no power
        no hope

impossible to contain
like wind and wave
it goes where it wills
and spreads like wild fire
when minds are open
to changing

everything looks different
once the veil is torn
and hands are on the plow

no looking back
only holding on
to the possibility of life
abundantly given

just beware of the cost:
    once you dance in the wind
    there is no returning
    and the world may not recognize
    the One whom you serve

> He said to him the third time, "Simon son of John, do you love
> me?" Peter felt hurt because he said to him the third time, "Do
> you love me?" And he said to him, "Lord, you know everything;
> you know that I love you." Jesus said to him, "Feed my sheep."
> John 21:17

PASTOR

Simon, son of John,
your love for Christ was never in question
perhaps you needed to speak the words
to accept forgiveness for impulsive, human denial
Jesus chose you to feed the flock that would
gather long after he was no longer quite so visibly present

Simon, Caiaphas, Peter
many names to describe the rock on which Christ
built the church that still stands today
even with your passionate, impetuous nature
your love and service reaches down through
centuries providing a model for all of us
who are called to feed the hungry who come
seeking what only Christ can give

Peter, every servant of Christ
should have your zeal and desire
to love and serve with nothing held back
you proclaimed Christ as messiah when others were
reluctant to see the God in the man who loved them
you wanted to protect him from the agony
he surely knew was coming
even in your weak moment of denial
you served him by saving your own life

You once walked on water until fear
overwhelmed you and Jesus saved you
from yourself, giving you the courage
to continue on the path of servanthood
Jesus named you friend and loved you as
you loved him enough to give your life
to feeding his sheep

Now all of us who answer the same call
to love and nurture those who belong to Christ
can stand with you, embodying the same
love and desire to spread the Gospel
with passion and conviction
even when our own impulsive humanity
might get in the way
like you we can trust that Christ
will save us from ourselves

May all of us who are called into ministry
have the courage and fire of Peter
to answer Christ's question,
"Do you love me?"
with Peter's answer,
"Lord, you know that I do."
And then go, feed the people of God
with grace and perseverance

> Peace I leave with you; my peace I give to you. I do not give to you
> as the world gives. Do not let your hearts be troubled, and do not
> let them be afraid.
> John 14:27

PEACE

an internal sense
of wellness in all   life
even when chaos flies freely   a quiet hope
for the world to one day see   the sacred
in all humanity resulting in respectful living with
one another opening to the possibility that
there are enough resources to sustain
everyone if we share across borders
made by human hands to those in
need of food, water, shelter, medication, fuel and
other things less tangible yet easier to
offer making all things well including
that small   fragile place in
our   own soul that
tells us what
is truly
good

And suddenly from heaven there came a sound like the rush of a
violent wind, and it filled the entire house where they were sitting.
Divided tongues, as of fire, appeared among them, and a tongue
rested on each of them. All of them were filled with the Holy Spirit
and began to speak in other languages, as the Spirit gave them
ability.
Acts 2:2–4

PENTECOST

Jesus promised the coming of Another
and still none were fully prepared
for the day the Spirit blew through
them, setting them on fire
filling them with the Word

accusations of drunkenness and insanity
were made by way of explanation by
those who did not have ears to hear
or eyes to see the Holy Spirit,
the Advocate Jesus bespoke

from that inexplicable day
the Church was born of wind
and flame and Word
that spread across the world
before anyone could have guessed
the power and strength on display

we have maybe forgotten the intensity
as we often pray,
"Come, Holy Spirit, Come"
without thinking about who
or what we invite to respond to our words

Barefoot Theology

we so discredit this Advocate by naming
the longest season of the Church year
"Ordinary Time" as if anything of the Spirit
could possibly be mundane

how would it be if today the Holy Spirit
responded to our invitations and came anew—
blew the doors off our sanctuaries
lit our heads on fire
and filled our mouths with the Word
for all to see and hear?

maybe we should act as if we
believe this is possible
just in case it's faith
that is needed

I in them and you in me, that they may become completely one,
so that the world may know that you have sent me and have loved
them even as you have loved me.
John 17:23

PERICHORESIS

Something within me denies my arrhythmic feet.

    A voice challenges:

        DANCE!

    Follow the steps of falling snow,
        the sway of new flowers,
        the fury of the sea,
        the whirl of autumn leaves.

        DANCE!

          Dance
            freedom
              courage
                transformation
                life

        DANCE!

Grant rhythm to my rooted feet, O Lord,

    So the whispers of my dreams
        stir my spirit
        set my blood tapping
        create an ache for

Barefoot Theology

> life
> freedom
> deep within

that I may evermore

DANCE!

with you.

Therefore, since we are surrounded by so great a cloud of witnesses, let us also lay aside every weight and the sin that clings so
closely, and let us run with perseverance the race that is set before
us . . .
Hebrews 12:1

PERSEVERANCE

Sun-golden
    persisting
        through the sidewalk

           Where are you now,
           regal rose?

           Planted in your manicured gardens—
           never venturing beyond the fences,
           never rooting in forbidden ground?

Look at this dandelion:
    No thorns or
        beauty to protect her

She turns her face upward
    to challenge
        the many feet

Give liberally and be ungrudging when you do so, for on this account the Lord your God will bless you in all your work and in all that you undertake. Since there will never cease to be some in need on the earth, I therefore command you, "Open your hand to the poor and needy neighbor in your land."
Deuteronomy 15:10–11

POVERTY

poor
broke
needy
destitute
people we want to
forget live right next door to us
we blame them for their situations making it more
likely that we will turn away and enjoy our things without giving
much thought to how
we share responsibility to help those in need
without passing judgment we must
give generously
knowing all
are loved
by
God

Likewise the Spirit helps us in our weakness; for we do not know
how to pray as we ought, but that very Spirit intercedes with sighs
too deep for words.
Romans 8:26

PRAYER

a conversation with God
takes many forms
      spoken and unspoken
      intentional and spontaneous
      contemplative and expletive
      articulated and imaged
      private and communal
      intercessory and thankful

in a grand cathedral or a humble chapel
out in the world or around the dining room table
hands clasped or raised or holding another
makes no difference to the One who listens
to hearts more than our heads
and responds in answer to our needs

nothing goes unanswered, not even gratitude
we may fail to notice until we look back
at where we've been to recognize
Grace was in that place

for those moments when all our words and deeds
fail to communicate the our deepest longings
the Holy Spirit will breathe them
into the heart of God
until we can say with all the saints,
"It is well with my soul"

> When the disciples heard this, they were greatly astounded and said, "Then who can be saved?" But Jesus looked at them and said, "For mortals it is impossible, but for God all things are possible."
> Matthew 19:25–26

PREDESTINATION

A child born innocent and beautiful
takes her first breath
and coughs out her first cry
God who may know the days of her life
wants only grace and mercy
to follow her

Others will touch her life with goodness
or with evil so she may not know the love
intended for her or hear a Word
that can drive away her despair
even if she is destined for salvation
she may lose her way

God's steadfast love will embrace her
when she feels forgotten
yet she may never turn to see the light
that shines in her and around her
will God save her anyway?

The ways of God are a mystery
we would do well to remember
that what is impossible for us
is possible for God
even if we wish otherwise

the question of who is destined for salvation
is less important than searching
for Christ in all those we encounter
as well as in ourselves

Let God worry about our final destiny
while we focus on living as if all
will be our neighbors through eternity

> Then I heard the voice of the Lord saying, "Whom shall I send,
> and who will go for us?" And I said, "Here am I; send me!"
> Isaiah 6:8

PROPHET

Moses, Isaiah, Jeremiah, Amos, Hosea and
many others whose names we recognize
risked everything to relay a message
to the wandering people of God
who did not welcome the call
to repent or the predictions of devastation
resulting from sin piled on sin
in the captivity of lesser gods
who made them all forget the God
whose breath fills their lungs
and will gather them all
and call them by name once more

These were the men of old who responded
to God's claim on their lives with a sometimes
reluctant "here am I" going where
God sent them to deliver news of
destruction or restoration depending
on the circumstances

What of today?
Surely there are no prophets running around
credibly predicting the end of the world
or the ruination of God's people
all the while claiming to quote God
word for word?

We are still a wandering people

those of us who make up the body of Christ
easily losing the path of grace
when confronted with other ways less
demanding than the church

There may not be a voice calling in the wilderness
though I've heard more than one prediction
of the church dying out while clinging to ways
that no longer glorify God or
bring salvation to the people

Prophets walk among us today
hidden in the many who cry out
their messages are the ones that unsettle
us and make our pews less comfortable
with a call to change our ways
to the point of replacing our pews
with couches and chairs
or worshiping outside of our buildings
altogether speaking a language
of change and transformation
that hits too close to home

Unlike those biblical days of yore
most who hear prophetic words
don't believe the church will cease to be
or that the price for our arrogance could be
a scattering of God's people

Of course, the others with prophetic
wisdom promise a time when we
will all be gathered in
to share in the harvest
if we would only listen
and change our ways

Barefoot Theology

God will build up the Body of Christ
into a new and unexpected shape

Let us pay heed to those disquieting voices
and listen attentively to those who speak
the Word even when no one wants to hear

Q

Without any doubt, the mystery of our religion is great: He was revealed in flesh, vindicated in spirit, seen by angels, proclaimed among Gentiles, believed in throughout the world, taken up in glory.
1 Timothy 3:16

QUESTIONS

Mostly it's about the whys
the questions that cause sighs
deep in my being, wordless
yearnings for answers beyond
grasping

grasping
hands reach out to comfort
and come up empty
doubts slither, slide into shadows
to return when silence
reaching

Barefoot Theology

reaching
out into the world and back again
to ask "Why, O Lord, why?"
tears flow or angry words burst
until I am still
knowing

knowing
better than my name
a simple truth provides no answers
just the capacity to choose
equally good or evil
feeling

feeling
effects of brokenness means
my own choice for apathy
or compassion, indifference
or action beyond
asking

asking
to be reminded of Your choices
steadfast, faithful to humanity
always desiring more for us
than we think possible
loving

loving
through the broken, violent,
destructive ways into new life
sacrificing yourself to give us
a choice to discover goodness,
to ask why and be still
waiting

waiting
for grace to shine through
sharp edges, soothing sadness
healing heartbreak, making
mercy alive in me
hoping

The Lord is my shepherd, I shall not want. He makes me lie down in green pastures; he leads me beside still waters; he restores my soul. He leads me in right paths for his name's sake.
Psalm 23:1–3

QUIET

In the murky blue light of the gloaming
a stillness washes over sleeping souls
while I emerge from dreaming to go roaming
beyond the confines of home and controls
of routine expectation. Seeking rest
that sleep does not provide, I turn east
toward the ocean's rhythms; morning's best
for spirit soothing solitude. Released
from all worry and distraction, moment
by moment I become part of the scene.
As the tide recedes, gulls cry atonement,
waves wash away yesterday, leaving clean,
untouched beach for the rising of the sun.
Calmed, I know the love of the Holy One.

R

For in him all the fullness of God was pleased to dwell, and
through him God was pleased to reconcile to himself all things,
whether on earth or in heaven, by making peace through the
blood of his cross.
Colossians 1:19–20

RECONCILIATION

years ago, more than I'd care to admit,
I was studying to be a minister
seeking God's love and approval
    in the basement of a church
    echoing with youth group voices
    from a meeting just ended
        my self-understanding shifted
        later than you would think
        in the life of one called to serve

a single moment of awakening
to a truth I'd always dismissed
as not really meant for me

Barefoot Theology

I was overwhelmed by where I had been
questioned where Christ was hiding
during the really hard times
    my assumption had always been absence
    because I was not good enough
    to be included in the love God so has for the world
    no matter how much I wanted to be
    or how hard I tried to make up for everything

Yet in that moment of pain and confession
when I was brave enough to speak out loud my fear
of being unforgivable and unworthy
while the friend who listened was wise enough
to keep quiet and let the Spirit lead
as Truth washed over me with power and certainty
like the tide rushing in to clean away debris
    I knew where Christ had been as clearly
    as I knew where I had been
    Jesus had been with me all along
        through the unbearable pain
        to the possibility of hope
        reaching out to me with many hands
        waiting for the day when
        Love would not be outside my reach

Jesus died for me and you and the whole world
so there would be no doubts about how God
views the world right down to the specifics
of me and you and the stranger walking by

He destined us for adoption as his children through Jesus Christ, according to the good pleasure of his will, to the praise of his glorious grace that he freely bestowed on us in the Beloved. In him we have redemption through his blood, the forgiveness of our trespasses, according to the riches of his grace that he lavished on us.
Ephesians 1:5–8

REDEMPTION

My journey began when we landed in Greece.
I sought You in Athens and Corinth,
then high up in the Parthenon, on the Acropolis.
When I didn't find You anywhere near,
I turned my hopes toward Israel, the Holy Land.
We boarded a bus in Tel Aviv and sang
of Your presence in this holy place and in our holy hands.
Thirty-four voices could not be wrong.
I expected to see You everywhere we went
in the Holy Land, from Tel Aviv to Messada.
Where else would You be during Lent?
When I didn't find You in the holy places,
I thought I'd missed You in the crowds.
When the sun shone with warm spring
and when Jerusalem was covered in clouds,
I searched for You—from Galilee to Bethlehem.
If not on the streets of these sacred cities,
then surely in the desert, mountains, gardens.
In Cana wedding vows were renewed with ease
and I felt Your hand heavy upon me.
So too on the Mount of Beatitudes and in Rachael's tomb.
My tears flowed in these places—cleansing,
washing away my sins and healing old wounds.
I knew You were creating in me a clean heart.
In the Holocaust museum I saw traces

of You in the millions of lights and heard
Rachael weeping for her children in this place
and I knew Your hands held many wounded souls.
But I heard only echoes of Your voice; I did not see
You in this remembering place. Later whispers of Your
name blew through branches in Gethsemane.
My tears fell in this garden where you cried
so many centuries ago. I looked up too late
to see You, though I felt Your presence.
The Via Delorosa, the Western Wall, and the Golden Gate
vibrated with your light, but I saw only
shadows of what I hoped for, prayed for.
Through us and for us—Pilgrims on a journey—
bread was broken and wine was poured.
I didn't find you there—not in the Cathedral,
on the Mount, or in the Garden—though I knew
You were there. Later, when our pilgrimage neared
the end, five of us gathered in honor of You
to break bread with a dying man. I saw
You there as I held the chalice to his lips
and he looked at me with Your eyes.
This man knew his future as he took a sip
of wine and joyously shared this simple meal
with me and those he loved. You held him
up in my Athens' dream and he showed me
Your face in a quiet moment, hidden in dim
light, wrapped in sacred space. In a hotel
room, I saw You face to face and I cried
for love of You. I should have known
You would take human form and not tried
to find You in ancient ruins or mosaics
on a wall. I should have looked for you in new
friends and old. Just the same I thank You
for showing me what I already knew
and for the moment when peace welled
up within me and wholeness blazed through

R

the dark places of my life. Bless the man
who looked at me with your eyes. You
and I met spirit to Spirit and now I am free.

Since many have undertaken to set down an orderly account of the
events that have been fulfilled among us, just as they were handed
on to us by those who from the beginning were eyewitnesses and
servants of the word, I too decided, after investigating everything
carefully from the very first, to write an orderly account for you,
most excellent Theophilus, so that you may know the truth con-
cerning the things about which you have been instructed.
Luke 1:1–4

REDACTION

Pay
close
attention,
dear reader,
to what is written,
by whom, and why

Look for the clues in themes,
motifs, vocabulary, and style

Compare to other accounts of the same event
to see what is added or removed to make a point

Remember to look at the Greek, Hebrew
or Aramaic before drawing any conclusions

These are good tools to use lest we forget that
every writer has an agenda, a goal, a reason
to spin a story in a certain direction,
especially when politics and
religion are twisted together
like they were in the
church's very
early days

as they
now
are

> Just so, I tell you, there will be more joy in heaven over one sinner
> who repents than over ninety-nine righteous persons who need
> no repentance.
> Luke 15:7

REPENTANCE

Not as easy as you might think to change one's ways
with a truly contrite heart

Depending on how far from the path you've wandered
it can be a long journey back
with a few more stumbles thrown in
to make sure you really want to change
your heart, mind, and actions

How many times can I confess my sins,
know I am forgiven, intend to start off in a new direction
as soon as the sun rises
only to find myself sinning again
with enthusiasm
until shame or guilt
kick me to the ground
and I beg for mercy once more?

As many times as it takes
before I can walk with God for a step
or two without wandering off down the same
path that leads me astray every time
I will be forgiven
when I come to God
pouring out my disgrace
opening myself to receive grace
enough to try again

Something will always lure me away into the dessert
or wilderness of the false promises and temporary bliss
To turn away from God is never my intent
when I find myself in disillusioned darkness
I have only to turn back to the Light
that no darkness can extinguish
and know that I will receive
mercy for another day
I only need to ask

Your word is a lamp to my feet and a light to my path.
Ps. 119:105

RELIGION

a framework to build our relationship with sacred mystery,
    shaping paths of love,
hope, justice, joy and peace for those seeking more from life
the way means less than the impact
on the travelers
who ought to
reveal
God's
grace

But strive first for the kingdom of God and his righteousness, and
all these things will be given to you as well.
Matthew 6:33

RIGHTEOUSNESS

Quoting scripture chapter and verse isn't something I can do
though I've read the Bible cover to cover more than once
I don't always make it to church on Sunday morning
nor do I sing loud enough for anyone other than God to hear
My offerings don't reach the ten percent of biblical mandate
On occasion I use words that aren't acceptable

Sometimes I look around and envy grabs me
I want the pretty, shiny trinkets others have
or I think how great it would be to win a Pulitzer
It isn't that I'm dissatisfied with life
occasionally I'm distracted by things that don't really matter

I forget that conforming to the views of others
as well as glitter and glamour don't mean much
when compared to service and justice
for those whom the world doesn't overly value
sacrificing a bit of my comfort to improve
the life of another even if no ever one notices

> . . . then the Lord God formed man from the dust of the ground, and breathed into his nostrils the breath of life; and the man became a living being.
> Genesis 2:7

RUACH

breathe
breathe again
simple inhale
exhale

focus
here now
quiet rest
undisturbed

present
in the sun
in the shadow
in the flower blooming

breathe in
breathe out
relax
be still
and know

S

Then he said to them, "The sabbath was made for humankind, and not humankind for the sabbath; so the Son of Man is lord even of the sabbath."
Mark 2:27–28

SABBATH

one
  day or
    a few hours
      of renewing
        rest reconnecting
          the human spirit with
            the Holy Spirit to breathe
              new life into tired souls giving
                creative possibility a
                  chance to reshape life from the inside out

> Make a joyful noise to the Lord, all the earth. Worship the Lord
> with gladness; come into his presence with singing. Know that
> the Lord is God. It is he that made us, and we are his; we are his
> people, and the sheep of his pasture. Enter his gates with thanks-
> giving, and his courts with praise. Give thanks to him, bless his
> name. For the Lord is good; his steadfast love endures forever, and
> his faithfulness to all generations.
> Psalm 100

SACRAMENT

Simple acts to remind us of God's claim on our lives

Water to wash away a life without Christ
Bread and wine draws us to a table set in love, calling us to love

We all agree on these two, yet there are more . . .

Two or seven matters less than participating in grace
revealed outwardly to humble and unite us all
in God's presence
available to all who come seeking—
saints, sinners, and all the rest who live in between

> Bathe in baptismal waters
> publically accept responsibility for these vows
> eat at Christ's table
> face your sins in the company of another
> receive God's blessing in union with your love
> dedicate your life to holy service
> anoint into grace those who face death

Do any or all of these mindful
of the visible signs of God's grace

And you, child, will be called the prophet of the Most High; for you will go before the Lord to prepare his ways, to give knowledge of salvation to his people by the forgiveness of their sins. By the tender mercy of our God, the dawn from on high will break upon us, to give light to those who sit in darkness and in the shadow of death, to guide our feet into the way of peace.
Luke 1:76–79

SALVATION

We have the knowledge
given to us in Christ
our sins are forgiven
we are saved

Worrying about it
changes nothing
assures us of even less
Christ came into the world
granting eternal life to all who believe

Simple

Then why are so many sitting in darkness
wondering why there is no way of peace?

Truth is only God knows who is saved
any energy we put into judging others
or proving our own place in eternal life
contradicts the promise that Christ's
love is for all

Simple

Barefoot Theology

Let us all live this gift freely given
put our efforts into living in this eternal love
extinguishing darkness
placing our feet firmly on the way of peace

Salvation happened on hill called Calvary

Simple

Our sins are forgiven
faith has saved us
Let us go in peace

He is the source of your life in Christ Jesus, who became for us
wisdom from God, and righteousness and sanctification and
redemption . . .
1 Corinthians 1:30

SANCTIFICATION

Shore
  Wind
    tears
      back
        hair
          rips
            into
              clothes

             I stand open

             Pull away
                  Submerge
               Autumn
              Clothes fall

       I plunge and swim

           Enveloped
           Sustained

           Naked strokes
            against the tide
              fight wave
                after wave

Barefoot Theology

Exhaustion
Surrender

Floating under
stars above
wind driving waves
I give thanks
I am home
in Grace

Come
Holy Spirit
Come

sun rises
I swim again

courage
submission
no struggle

only Love
more fully myself
in the fullness of Christ

Humble yourselves therefore under the mighty hand of God, so that he may exalt you in due time. Cast all your anxiety on him, because he cares for you. Discipline yourselves, keep alert. Like a roaring lion your adversary the devil prowls around, looking for someone to devour. Resist him, steadfast in your faith, for you know that your brothers and sisters in all the world are undergoing the same kinds of suffering.
1 Peter 5:6–9

SATAN

No horns, pitchfork, or pointy tail
evil is not incarnate the way Love is
yet often enough it seems to be

War, murder, mass shootings, hate crimes,
rape, sickness unto death, inexplicable
human acts

To put the blame on demons may be convenient scapegoats
for those avoiding responsibility
for violent, destructive actions
or other inexplicable things

Satan may have fallen from heaven in a lightning flash
but it's human beings that commit horrific crimes
or refuse to accept a role in
global warming and super storms,
drought, poverty, and hungry children,
the possibility of pandemic flu,
untreated mental illness,
homeless families
and more

Barefoot Theology

The world is not as God intended it to be
we often make choices God would rather we did not

I've run into evil in this world with certainty
I've just never seen it without a human face

Your word is a lamp to my feet and a light to my path.
Psalm 119:105

SCRIPTURE

A sacred text, the word of God
All religions have some
and all believe they contain
revelations from their God
Christians have the Bible
even though they don't agree
on much about it

Some claim it is the inerrant Word of God
even though they don't observe every law
or try to reconcile the discrepancies
Others say it is divinely inspired,
written by men, not quite perfect

When it comes down to the ink on the page,
the Bible tells us far more about what it is to be human—
our weaknesses, our fears, our needs—
than it ever says about God

From Genesis through Revelation
Truth is revealed for those who seek it
while not everything is really true

Read it with an open mind, remembering
that English was not a language when it was written
and it's been translated and mistranslated many times
while the message remains the same

Barefoot Theology

It's not a history book, or even a single book,
rather a collection of stories written by peoples
as they search for the God who loves them
and yearns to be to be known

Or do you not know that your body is a temple of the Holy Spirit within you, which you have from God, and that you are not your own? For you were bought with a price; therefore glorify God in your body.

1 Corinthians 6:19–20

SEXUALITY

a gift, a blessing easily misunderstood,
misused, abused, ignored, denied, repressed
an essential part of being human
a physicality sometimes exploited
by assumptions of normality
when normal means almost nothing
in the face of individual particularities

our bodies were never meant to be a source of shame
more a source of pleasure, delight
a reflection of our maker's endless creativity
and means of expressing ourselves in the world

if we live recognizing our bodies as holy
seeing others as sacred
places in which the Holy Spirit is pleased to dwell,
accepting ourselves, respecting others
becomes sacred responsibility

In you, O Lord, I seek refuge; do not let me ever be put to shame;
in your righteousness deliver me. Incline your ear to me; rescue
me speedily. Be a rock of refuge for me, a strong fortress to save
me. You are indeed my rock and my fortress; for your name's sake
lead me and guide me, take me out of the net that is hidden for
me, for you are my refuge. Into your hand I commit my spirit; you
have redeemed me, O Lord, faithful God.
Psalm 31:1–6

SHAME

dark fingers wrapping around the self
shaping perceptions
preventing the fullness of life
often for no reason beyond
misplaced responsibility

humiliation that comes from within
gains strength the longer it sits
in darkness
feeding on fear, waiting for more

the only way to freedom
is to expose the pain to the Light
remove the power from those choking
shadowy hands
with words spoken loud enough
for another to hear
and speak words of absolution,
forgiveness, healing
allowing hidden wounds to heal

The Lord created me at the beginning of his work, the first of
his acts of long ago. Ages ago I was set up, at the first, before the
beginning of the earth.
Proverbs 8:22–23

SOPHIA

By way of warning I must say
  that I've been known to sit at Sophia's feet—
    the Goddess within the God—
      the still, small voice in the dark of night
      brings light to my path and
      melody to my dance.

      Hovering over creation waters
      Wisdom gave birth to dry land.
      Later she spoke the Word become flesh.
      In between
        She held Eve's hand at the gates of Eden
        Taught Sarah to laugh
          and Miriam to dance.
        She gave comfort to Hagar
          and courage to Esther.

      And one night she sat with Mary
        who pondered a request
      Sophia held her hand in those moments
        between her yes and possible no.
        Then they walked together for
        nine months that spread beyond thirty years.

    She danced with others, too—
      a woman at a well who yearned
        for living water

had the Wisdom to ask for a drink.

Another who poured out oil and tears
   in search of life
     found Wisdom on her knees
   before the Word spoken aloud.

And let us not forget the other Mary—
the one of questionable means—
She danced with grace that only Sophia could grant—
   demons cast out and
     sins forgiven—
   Compassion rooted in her soul; she found
     hope in Wisdom's child as her
       eyes were opened.

There are others more numerous than those in the Book—
Daughters of Sophia—I am one, perhaps you as well . . .

Eyes wide with wonder I see her:
   forgotten Goddess swallowed in
     memory of the God.

Lest we forget,
   She holds the world in her hands
   By her light we see
   By her guidance we live—
   at least we try . . .

You need not agree;
   just remember I sit at Sophia's feet
     and listen for a voice seldom heard . . .

Therefore God also highly exalted him and gave him the name
that is above every name, so that at the name of Jesus every knee
should bend, in heaven and on earth and under the earth, and
every tongue should confess that Jesus Christ is Lord, to the glory
of God the Father. Therefore, my beloved, just as you have always
obeyed me, not only in my presence, but much more now in my
absence, work out your own salvation with fear and trembling; for
it is God who is at work in you, enabling you both to will and to
work for his good pleasure.
Philippians 2:9–13

SOTERIOLOGY

Studying salvation and all its doctrines
is not unreasonable, a worthy use of time
and energy to understand saving theology as it is
written in scriptures and other books

Learning the views of others, discovering wisdom
in words recorded for the sake of the next generation
enriches the student as long as the study does not
end with words on someone else's pages

Being saved means living now, working out
our own salvation with fear and trembling, trusting
God's grace includes all who reach out in faith,
leaving the ultimate decision in hands holier than our own

Barefoot Theology

> . . . the fruit of the Spirit is love, joy, peace, patience, kindness, generosity, faithfulness, gentleness, and self-control. There is no law against such things.
> Galatians 5:22–23

SPIRITUALITY

something within me aches for more—
more
  love, joy, peace,
  patience, kindness, generosity,
  faithfulness, gentleness, self-control

hiking through the woods on an October day
or walking the beach on an August night
  stirs these things within me
  awakening a desire to create
   with words or paint
   images pointing to truths
    yet to be told

    fiery leaves
     cresting waves
      woodland smells
       salty air
    satisfy my soul for moments
    they are fleeting

unless I connect this temporary peace
to something greater
which will guide my passion
for life and connection
without which I would lose myself
in a search for more

150

my spirit yearns for the Holy—
those moments when all of life is balanced
in a promise of abundance

gratitude to the Creator of trees and seasons,
beaches and breezes,
will hold me in the days of imbalance
when longing is stronger than hope
until Love overflows once again

the One who commands love
soothes my soul

for others there may be Another
but without Christ
I lose my way

> Above all, maintain constant love for one another, for love covers a multitude of sins. Be hospitable to one another without complaining. Like good stewards of the manifold grace of God, serve one another with whatever gift each of you has received.
> 1 Peter 1:8–10

STEWARDSHIP

one
part
prayer
another faith
mostly gratitude
recognizing all that we have
belongs to God who entrusts us with many gifts
intending us to care for the whole of creation leaving nothing out
we are called to be faithful with all things large or small
wisely using all resources
to glorify God
in all things
body
and
soul

T

Blessed is anyone who endures temptation. Such a one has stood the test and will receive the crown of life that the Lord has promised to those who love him.

James 1:12

TEMPTATION

The Tempter showed up in the wilderness
hoping Jesus would forsake his God
    to eat and be satisfied
    to prove his power beyond argument
    to receive the world without effort
Jesus turned down all offers even after days of fasting
He knew what he would lose—
    himself and his God
        the relationship would be destroyed
        and the world would lose all hope

Consequently we can be reminded that Jesus
withstood the pain of facing the Tempter
He is acquainted with how seductive

    appetites can be
        avenues of escape
        promises of satiation
        false idols of fulfillment
He knows the enticement
    of great power
        illusions of control
        appearances of respect
        a mirage of being more worthy than others
He recognizes the dazzle
    of tremendous wealth
        a life of endless possibilities
        a way to fulfill every desire
        an implausible way to widen the needle's eye

The next time the Tempter pays a visit
talk to the Christ who has resisted
and can show us how to turn away
from all that would cost
more than we can afford to pay

Let us not forget that when the Tempter wins
Christ stands with the tormented soul
watching, waiting for a moment
to step in and open the door
to wholeness, forgiveness, and grace

But I say to you, Love your enemies and pray for those who perse-
cute you, so that you may be children of your Father in heaven; for
he makes his sun rise on the evil and on the good, and sends rain
on the righteous and on the unrighteous.
Matthew 5:44–45

THEODICY

Bad things happen to good people throughout all time.
The tendency to blame God for things really wrong
lies within us. Why would the One who created
us seek to do us harm? Thinking like this is senseless.
Surely, the time has come. Responsibility
is ours for destructive ways, disastrous choices,

and our propensity for violence—these choices
that human beings make without thought all the time
impacting more than we know. Responsibility
for evil's power lies with humanity. Wrong
ways of living and being don't appear senseless
until we look and see all the pain created

by selfishness, anger, pride, greed. We created
much of what is wrong in the world today. Choices
made by those with power to oppress brought senseless
hurt to innocents. Before we run out of time,
can we make changes, stop ignoring what is wrong?
The world is fragile. Our responsibility

to be good stewards, our responsibility
to care for each other is why God created
human beings. Yet we have freedom to choose wrong
over right. The effect of these selfish choices
often culminates in disaster at some time
for some guiltless other. To blame God is senseless

when humans have made many a foolish, senseless
decision. Surely, our responsibility
for the sickness of earth cannot be denied. Time
has shown the damage done. The One who created
all wants only that we live rightly, make choices
for the benefit of the whole creation. Wrong

living eventually leads to pain, and wrong
actions impact the world, opening to senseless
evil. God doesn't intervene in our choices
very often. To say responsibility
for evil belongs to the God who created
us in love, for love, defies reason. Isn't it time

to acknowledge the wrong? Responsibility
for evil lies in senseless actions. Created
in God's image, our choices can improve this time.

Six days later, Jesus took with him Peter and James and John, and led them up a high mountain apart, by themselves. And he was transfigured before them, and his clothes became dazzling white, such as no one on earth could bleach them.
Mark 9:2–3

THEOPHANY

Probably nothing so spectacular
as a mountain top transfiguration
still quite shocking to the traveler
going along without expectation

of a holy visitation. To see
God visible in the world is quite
startling even for the devotee
who is certain it would be cool to be

so clearly visited by the Holy
One. Yet, when our God breaks into the world,
transformation happens in the ones who see
as reality becomes a bit whorled.

God chooses the time and place to show
sacred power to those who need to know.

Jesus said to them, "I am the bread of life. Whoever comes to me will never be hungry, and whoever believes in me will never be thirsty."
John 6:35

TRADITION

Our faith is built on many practices
a rich history of people, places, prophets
point to Jesus as the way, the truth, and the life

No problems arise until we decide
that our branch of the Christian tree
is the only one and all others are damned

The whole of our history—from ancient days
to modern ways—is the foundation on which
the church stands . . . or falls

Trouble begins when we mistake human
devices for divine Truth, treating our rituals
as more sacred than all else

Jesus told his followers that all who come
to him will eat, drink, and be satisfied
we would do well to listen more closely

It's good to know our history of faith and practice
to understand how we came to be
the body of Christ here and now

It might be better to know when to let go
of what's no longer useful
to make room at the table for all who hunger and thirst

The grace of the Lord Jesus Christ, the love of God, and the communion of the Holy Spirit be with all of you.
2 Corinthians 13:14

TRINITY

Three equals one and one equals three—
the logic of Christianity—
confounds thinkers in modernity.

Whether the traditional Father,
Son, Holy Spirit or another
naming doesn't really much matter.

You need an encounter with the God
whose incarnate love will leave you awed
to make you forget that the math is flawed.

U

There is no longer Jew or Greek, there is no longer slave or free,
there is no longer male and female; for all of you are one in
Christ Jesus.
Galatians 3:28

UNCHURCHED

Long ago there were heathens and heresies abounding
of course those changed depending on whom you asked
though Christians of any stripe were sure of themselves
     and more sure of their God,
          their salvation,
               their righteousness.

               Over the centuries
               society has shifted
               the church out of the center
               more toward the periphery
               in all but our old towns.

Now most believers encounter more others
than ever before and have to question their own faith

language and communication to those who have none
not different or foreign, just no belief at all
except the traces that permeate society, remnants
of days long gone into an idealized past
that might be more wishful thinking than actual history.

Somehow, we who worship in pews on Sunday mornings
are responsible for the growing number of faithless ones.
Their parents or grandparents once worshipped side by side
with you or me and now they prefer not to don their Sunday best
and sing old hymns or practice ancient rituals whose meaning
may have been lost in one generation or another

In Christ all are sisters and brothers
    there aren't any others for the one who lives in Christ
        ought to view all—believers and unbelievers
        of all varieties—with the same Christian love

        Perhaps with more value placed on people
            less on Traditions and maintaining a mythic past
        more emphasis on embodying Jesus' profound love
            less on deciding who is right
            in thought, word, and deed
        fewer people would check none
        on the religious affiliation box
        and more would want to find their place
        in the body of Christ
        where all ought to be welcomed
        with extravagant hospitality
        and abundant grace

Because, after all, the church is still the people
even those who have yet to step over a threshold

Yes, everything is for your sake, so that grace, as it extends to more
and more people, may increase thanksgiving, to the glory of God.
So we do not lose heart. Even though our outer nature is wasting
away, our inner nature is being renewed day by day. For this slight
momentary affliction is preparing us for an eternal weight of glory
beyond all measure, because we look not at what can be seen but
at what cannot be seen; for what can be seen is temporary, but
what cannot be seen is eternal.
2 Corinthians 4:15–18

UNSEEN

Not the things we choose not to see—
 neighbors arguing behind open windows
 homeless children sleeping in doorways
 soldiers dying in an endless war
 politicians breaking too many promises
 nameless people suffering around the world

The things we forget to see—
 neighbors who love one another into old age
 children quickly making friends with a new child
 soldiers gently rebuilding war-ravaged lives
 politicians quietly advocating for justice
 unknown people willingly holding hands

What lies outside our view
could save us from despair
and rescue us from ourselves

It's the grace and beauty in our world
in each human being
the possibility of wonder, awe,
that old amazing grace
which never seems to make the news

and often goes unnoticed

    Autumn's first golden touch on green leaves
    Intricacies of snowflakes even in a blizzard
    Buds opening on a tree bent over with late-winter ice
    Endless summer sounds of creatures in hidden places

    Wonder filling a cynical heart as the sun rises
        setting the world on fire after a desperately dark night
    Joy touching the center of a grieving spirit as a rainbow
        colors the stormy sky in the company of another
    Hope grabbing the edges of life nearly lost as stars
        shoot across revealing the possibility of a new path
    Love overcoming a hate-filled soul as thunder
        echoes the promises of a cleansing storm

May our eyes be open
    to the mysteries of the Eternal
        especially when our view is clouded
            by things we do not wish to see

> Go and learn what this means, "I desire mercy, not sacrifice. For I
> have come to call not the righteous but sinners."
> Matthew 9:13

UNWORTHY

So many tearstained faces fill my days
crying out because they will never be good enough
for God to love them
They are bound up with shame forced on their
innocence and cannot see their way to freedom

I ask what they have done that is so sinful
These women, men, and children
only recount a list of evils done to them
held close by the pain they've inflicted
on their own bodies trying to be rid
of a hurt deeper than they can speak

Why do you think that God cannot love you
if you have committed no horrific sin?
All of them confess that they are worthless
yet they believe in Jesus,
that Jesus died to save the world

Yes! God so loved the world
without excluding you!
Would you give your life
for something without value?

They all agree that dying for something worthless
would be rather stupid and pointless
God so loved the world . . .
are you part of the world that God so loved?

Yes
Then you are not worthless
Jesus died for you as well as the rest of creation
Are you sure?

Absolutely!
Are you willing to tell God that a mistake has been made,
that you are outside the bounds of God's love for the whole world?

Well, when you put it that way
maybe I am wrong
maybe God loves me
maybe there is hope
maybe I am more than this collection of pain

Yes! We are, and always have been!

V

"Look, the virgin shall conceive and bear a son, and they shall name him Emmanuel," which means, "God is with us."
Matthew 1:23

VIRGIN BIRTH

The miracle does not lie with Mary's virginity
or taking this story of Jesus' birth literally
Rather with the fact that God became incarnate
and changed human history forever after

And still, there is more to the story
of a young girl agreeing to bear God
into the world at great cost to herself
and her loved ones

A teenage, unwed mother consented—
make no mistake, she was not forced
There was likely a long pause before her
"Let it be with me as you have said"

Mary agreed to bring Jesus into the world
and then she got out of the way
so that her story became Christ's story
with an invitation for us to do the same

May we all have the courage to bring
the Incarnate One into our world
then let our story become part of Christ's
on-going revelation of grace

W

"... but those who wait for the Lord shall renew their strength, they shall mount up with wings like eagles, they shall run and not be weary, they shall walk and not faint."
Isaiah 40:31

WAITING

Sarah's laughter echoes into her old age
finding prophecy fulfilled after it was
too late for her yet just on time for God
to make something happen when
everything seemed impossible

Isaiah after the wind, earthquake, and fire
stumbling into silence
breathing in the stillness
pausing before the journey resumes
in the midst of chaos

Gabriel surprising a young woman
with an invitation to bear God
into the world like no other
needed an answer before
proceeding

Mary spoke "let it be with me . . ."
and spent years standing between
joy and heartbreak
wrapped in grace
fully expecting

Peter in those moments after
sinking in the waves
watching blood pour from a servant's ear
denying Jesus on impulse
anticipating condemnation

Jesus in the garden, on the cross, in the tomb
wanting something else
in his tears, his pain, his death
alone as no others have been
fulfilling prophecy, promise beyond knowing

All who live between
darkness and light
sickness and healing
despair and hope
shame and forgiveness

Come, Holy Spirit, come

Then the angel showed me the river of the water of life, bright as crystal, flowing from the throne of God and of the Lamb through the middle of the street of the city. On either side of the river is the tree of life with its twelve kinds of fruit, producing its fruit each month; and the leaves of the tree are for the healing of the nations.
Revelation 22:1–5

WATER

necessary for all life on earth—human, plant, animal, even bug—
too often
    taken for granted and misused by those who've never
    gone without, not ever thinking
        about those who thirst
            for waters
                that won't
                    flow

                 Christ
               offered
            an outcast
        living water from
     a well deeper than possible
  for the human mind to imagine but the spirit
yearns to drink without ceasing, to be filled to overflowing—grace
freely poured for all

in the desert, wilderness, city, or farm, the River of Life feeds the
Tree of Life
    offering leaves for the healing of all the nations
        we are poor stewards of water
            how will we ever
                embody

Christ's love
more

more
than we
whose thirst seems
endless can possibly become
God who so loved the world invites us to drink deeply
quench our thirst pass the cup of Living Water from one
parched soul to another freely

given water enough for all living creatures to drink deeply and be
satisfied
when the River of Life flows freely nations will
heal hatred will end peace will reign
how you and I live
matters don't
spill a
drop

> The whole congregation of the Israelites complained against Moses and Aaron in the wilderness.
> Exodus 16:2

WILDERNESS

a place of necessity
though often unwanted
unexpected
unnerving

Moses led God's people
through a time of hunger, thirst, and despair
for forty years until they were ready
to experience the Promised land

I have often lost my way
only to discover I'd stepped off the path
into the chaos of doubt and despair
complaining instead of praying

I remain in that desolate place
searching desperately for a way out
until I encounter God whose
been beside me all along

When I've looked up from my misery
to see that a way has been made clear
I can cross from captivity to freedom
not for the first time or the last

Sometimes we need to journey
through untamed lands where fear
and darkness live in order to leave
our captors in the past

The Israelites needed forty years
to let go of expectations and anxieties
enough to remember that God is with us
even in the empty, barren places

a place of necessity
though often unwanted
unexpected, unnerving
where we are fully exposed to our need for God

X

Let mutual love continue. Do not neglect to show hospitality to strangers, for by doing that some have entertained angels without knowing it.
Hebrews 13:1–2

XENOPHOBIA

fear and hatred of those unknown to us
        has no place in Christian living
to reject another for familiar reasons—
        skin color, country of origin,
        religious practice, sexual orientation,
        gender identity, economic status
        and all the other ways we dismiss
        those who differ from us—
is contrary to all God's ways.

Would Isaac ever have been born if Abraham
        turned away those visitors
        who promised Sarah would conceive?

How many young women turned Gabriel away
          before Mary consented to bear Christ into the world?

How might our lives be blessed if we treated all as sacred guests?

Jesus journeyed to the margins
          touched the people living there
          and drew them into new life

Jesus was fearless enough to touch
          the unclean, the outcast, the broken
and make them whole
powerfully enough
to reach through the ages
asking that we who bear the name of Christ
do the same

erase the margins
bring the outcast
in Christ we are one

Y

God said to Moses, "I am who I am." He said further, "Thus you shall say to the Israelites, 'I am has sent me to you.'"
Exodus 3:14

YHWH

The God who just is.
If it were only that simple . . .

Once upon a time, it was.
Time and tradition have convoluted
the simplicity of a straight forward revelation.

Over the generation vowels have been lost
leaving us to guess at the pronunciation
not to mention the nature of the One who really Is.
An effort at piety and respect of the Holy taken to extreme
distanced the people from God to the point
where Another was sent to claim the title.
Jesus embodied the I Am fully:

light of the world
the One before Abraham even existed
the gate to salvation
the good shepherd who lays down his life
the resurrection and the life
the way, the truth, and the life
the true vine apart from which there is no life
the One before whom even soldiers fall

Let us not bury this One who is, who was, and is to come
in unnecessary pious traditions lest we forget
how to speak the Holy Name

Have you not known? Have you not heard? The Lord is the ever-lasting God, the Creator of the ends of the earth. He does not faint or grow weary; his understanding is unsearchable. He gives power to the faint, and strengthens the powerless. Even youths will faint and be weary, and the young will fall exhausted; but those who wait for the Lord shall renew their strength, they shall mount up with wings like eagles, they shall run and not be weary, they shall walk and not faint.

Isaiah 40:28–31

YOUTH

I stand at the mirror wondering at the woman I see
    gray streaks through her hair
    crows have left footprints around her eyes
    wrinkles beginning to slide down her neck
    the hand the reaches up to push hair aside
    belongs to a woman older than I feel
where did she come from

    this woman
        no longer young
        yet not quite old
    has my eyes
        squint lines etched between them

I stand, staring, trying to remember
    where all the days and years have gone
        was not yesterday filled with
            yearning to grow up
            hating not being old enough
            thinking myself not good enough

now here I am with youth behind me
    revealing strength unexpected

passion, humor, wisdom
live in those reflected eyes

no, I would not turn back time
   nor erase the marks of its passing
I will not worship the idol of youthful appearance
   my scars and imperfections tell of my broken places
      where healing is

   most value the flimsy
      transient beauty of youth
      yet who wants to recapture
         those days of unappreciated innocence
            serious about everything
            foolishly reaching for illusions

even now, I am haunted by some of those false images
   I would trade nothing to begin again
   return those days when I did not fit in my own skin

I have earned these growing wrinkles
   stretching my limits and reaching beyond the obvious

   my running days may be over
      but I am still walking
         away from the weariness of always wanting more

my artist's eyes are open to all possibilities
   now that I am old enough to see how
   beauty and suffering weave together in wonder

my poet's ears hear the Word of life
   in unexpected places, always whispering,
    "I have called you by name and you are mine"
   spoken long before I had ears to hear

Barefoot Theology

        youth passes quickly, quietly,
        unnoticed until it is too late to say goodbye

          to chase after those reckless days
        means missing the wonderment of today
    failing to recognize that I am
fearfully, wonderfully made

decades stack up
    gratitude fills me
        made of sturdier things
           the youth I possess now will not fade

          I wait for the Lord

that face in the mirror, smiles
thinking of the day when she will soar with eagles

Z

Do not lag in zeal, be ardent in spirit, serve the Lord.
Romans 12:11

ZEAL

Don't throw reason out the proverbial window
but let joyful passion guide where the faithful go.
Why do as always has been done, when so much waits
for us to explore? Why let tradition dictate
so much of how the church embodies Christ today?

Revelation cautions with some wise words to say
it's much better to be hot or cold than lukewarm
danger awaits any who try too hard to conform
the risk is being spit out of the mouth of Christ.

Half-hearted faith, lame motions, never sufficed
in spite of what we tell ourselves. Our God desires
followers to burn with unquenchable fires.

Yes, doubts may come, but Christianity should bore
none. Isn't ambivalence what we should abhor?

Scripture Index